15

SUNANDA PATWARDHAN

A Vision
of the
Sacred:

My Personal
Journey
with
Krishnamurti

EDWIN HOUSE PUBLISHING, INC.

A VISION OF THE SACRED:
MY PERSONAL JOURNEY WITH KRISHNAMURTI
By Sunanda Patwardhan, Ph.D.

Published by Edwin House Publishing, Inc.
P. O. Box 128, Ojai, California 93024, USA

Edited by Malini Srinivasan, Ph.D.

Designed by Margaret Dodd
adapted from a design by Karen Davidson

Printed by Delta Direct Access, California, USA

10 9 8 7 6 5 4 3 2 1

Library of Congress Cataloging-in-Publication Data 99-71343

Patwardhan, Sunanda.

A vision of the sacred : my personal journey with
Krishnamurti / by Sunanda Patwardhan. – 1st ed.
p. cm.

ISBN: 0-9649-247-6-5

1. Krishnamurti, J. (Jiddu), 1895-
2. Patwardhan, Sunanda.   3. Spiritual biography—
India.   I. Title.

B5134.K75P38 1999   181'.4

QBI99-500434

CONTENTS

ACKNOWLEDGMENTS

I WOULD LIKE TO EXPRESS MY GRATITUDE AND APPRECIATION to my dear friend Malini Srinivasan who, despite her commitments, untiringly encouraged me to write this book. It is she who painstakingly read through the various drafts, and shaped and edited them with understanding and affection.

I especially thank R. E. Mark Lee for unhesitatingly taking on the responsibility of publishing this work.

I acknowledge the various friends and relatives who in their special ways have helped me through the last year.

Finally, my eternal gratitude to my husband and dear companion, who has been my constant strength and support in this journey to the sacred.

Sunanda Patwardhan

F O R E W O R D

DURING THE YEARS OF THE SECOND WORLD WAR, Krishnamurti, unable to travel, remained quietly in Ojai, California, giving no public talks. It was only in October 1947 that he again returned to India, where two months earlier, independence had been gained from British rule. He came alone and was greeted by old friends, but his presence soon attracted many young people. Among these was Sunanda, daughter of South Indian brahmanical parents and members of the Theosophical movement. She was twenty years old, newly graduated from Madras University. The meeting with Krishnamurti was a turning point, which began for her a lifetime of discovery in the light of his teaching. It was also an influence that shaped the outward direction of her life, and also, after her marriage two years later, that of her husband Pama Patwardhan.

Her response on meeting Krishnamurti was to see in him someone of a different order who had gone beyond the boundaries of familiar consciousness, and began immediately for her what she felt as a spiritual journey toward something sacred. Her plans for further academic studies were suspended and, with her parents' concurrence, she chose to follow Krishnamurti and his teaching. During the travels this entailed, in Pune she met Pama Patwardhan, a younger brother in a family that was close to Krishnamurti and also deeply involved in the political life of India. An older brother, Achyut Patwardhan, had known Krishnaji since 1928, and both he and another brother Rao had become national heroes in the fight for Indian independence. Pama took part in this as well.

After their marriage, both Sunanda and Pama remained deeply committed to Krishnaji, his teaching and the structure of his work in India. They were members of what became the Krishnamurti Foundation India and were central to its activities throughout their lives. From her first meeting with Krishnamurti in 1947 until her death in 1999, the path of Sunanda's life was seldom far from the activities of his work, but though she returned to academic pursuits and accomplishments for a time, the thread of inquiry, the search for something beyond the limits of common existence, a radiance she had perceived so eagerly in her youth, remained unbroken.

Throughout the years, the light of Krishnaji's guidance was there for her. It is this that is the content of her memoir. In recounting it, she offers the reader an eloquent record of what that was, of how she learned to meet conflict, sorrow and sickness, the meaning of awareness, of sensitivity, and above all the meaning of inward silence.

Krishnaji's affection and trust in Sunanda's essential direction and capacities took a hand in the direction of her and Pama's life. For years they lived in Delhi, where Pama was executive director of a leading publishing house, and Sunanda became responsible for the editing and publication of Krishnamurti material for KFI, but in 1975 their life took a turn and they left Delhi, with Krishnaji's approval, to live in Bangalore where Sunanda's parents were.

Krishnaji did not go to India that year. A state of emergency had been declared by Mrs. Gandhi and Krishnaji had remained in California, from where he wrote urging Sunanda and Pama to come to a scientists' conference in Ojai. A second letter revealed that he intended them to take over the care of Vasanta Vihar, which had not been available for his work due to legal difficulties. It had been acquired originally as the head-quarters in Madras for Krishnamurti, but this had been impossible until legal means placed it in a new trust. Sunanda and Pama moved there in July 1976. Pama was appointed secretary of Krishnamurti Foundation India and Vasanta Vihar became its headquarters. Together they under-took to make the neglected house and grounds suitable for Krishnaji and for his work. He wished it to be not only beautiful, but a religious place, and it was Sunanda's especial responsibility to bring this about. With the help of other friends devoted to him, the place was transformed in time for Krishnaji's arrival in December of that year for his public talks. From then on until 1986, his yearly visits illumined Vasanta Vihar and brought a tide of people who not only attended the talks but also took part in discussions, dialogues and seminars. It was Sunanda's responsibility to organize these, invite interesting participants and ultimately to edit the texts for publication.

Through the years, it was also Sunanda's custom to make notes of many informal conversations over the lunch table or elsewhere when serious exchanges with Krishnaji took place. In these ways, the many sides of Krishnaji's guidance are preserved through her account of his words of counsel to her as an individual through most of her life. The personal journey that Sunanda has written is an eloquent testimony of a life touched by Krishnamurti and the light of his teaching.

Major changes came in 1986. Before Krishnaji left India, he had accepted Sunanda and Pama's decision that it was time to relinquish their roles at Vasanta Vihar. His own health made it necessary to cut short his talks in India and return to California, where he died on February 17th.

Illness came to both Pama and Sunanda, and after four years in Madras, they decided to spend their remaining years in Pune, to which they moved in 1990. They had no plan for further activity on behalf of the Foundation, but events presented them with a major challenge. Achyut Patwardhan had long felt that there should be a Krishnamurti school on the west coast of India, and when in 1992 ninety acres on a beautiful hilltop not far from Pune was donated to KFI, the creation of a school was immediately begun. Three months later, the death of Achyut left the immense responsibility to Pama to not only find further financing, but to bring to the bare hilltop a road, power, water, structures, planting, and most importantly, the right people to create the school. This formidable task was accomplished by September 1995 when the Sahyadri School opened to students, where there are presently over two hundred.

Sunanda's part was supportive in all this, but she felt the urgency of Krishnaji's conviction that a Study Center for adults was intrinsic to every school and bringing this about became her deep-felt aim. The Sahyadri Study Center was formally inaugurated on November 29, 1998. This and the finishing of this book were the two tasks that Sunanda set to complete, in spite of profoundly failing health; a culmination of a life lived in a direction toward something she felt to be sacred. She died on the morning of February 25, 1999.

It was only after this that I learned that Sunanda had asked that I write a foreword to her book. I am both touched and honored that she should wish this. I do not know her reasons, but do know the sense of friendship and sharing of a central concern in both our lives: the teaching of Krishnamurti. And in memory for me there is always the gaiety, the human spirit, the warmth and courage of Sunanda.

Mary Zimbalist

PREFACE

IN THIS BOOK I PAY MY HOMAGE TO J. KRISHNAMURTI, WHO LEFT us in 1986. My association with him began on the day I met him in Madras in 1947, and I deeply cherish the affection and friendship I received during the many years I knew him. I am immeasurably indebted to him for helping me begin my inward journey and for awakening in me a vision of the sacred.

A vision of the sacred seems to be gathering a new emphasis today as the demands of our frenetic lifestyles have intensified our need for the spiritual. And we continuously ask questions about what lies beyond the phenomenal world.

Beyond the phenomenal lies the sacred, say seers like J. Krishnamurti (or Krishnaji, as he was affectionately called), who seem to have touched a shore outside our narrow experiences. Krishnaji has shown us the vibrant energy and creativity of a mind that has gone beyond the frontiers of conditioned consciousness. How was this sense of the sacred transmitted to those who had not such a vision? How did he communicate this sense of the sacred to individuals who were serious and wanted a feel of the timeless? His words, his very demeanor, revealed the compassionate radiance of a transformed mind and drew thousands to his presence. According to him, an understanding of our conditioning initiates a transforming process within consciousness. Through transcending our conditioning, we get a glimpse of a sacred way of life, which reveals to us the possibility of a transformation of our consciousness.

My writings describe the path I took to understand the pain, conflict, and impermanence of daily life. The narrative reveals how at certain significant moments in my life I met Krishnaji, and the ways in which he changed my life, my horizons and my perceptions. My involvement with the Krishnamurti Foundation India (KFI) and its activities also form part of this fabric. Inevitably the narrative is biographical and continuously reveals the thread between the teacher, the teaching, and the taught.

I have chosen to write this as a personal narrative, as it brings a sense of intimacy and transparency to the reader. In this conversation, there is a freedom in me to be unselfconscious and open in describing and sharing my innermost thoughts and experiences. I have traced the movement of my life chronologically from the time I met Krishnaji to the present day. The years after his passing away represent steps in my spiritual journey taken with great tentativeness, for there was no corroboration from the teacher. They have brought a measure of self-reliance and trust in one's perceptions as one walks hesitantly on an unsure path.

I N T R O D U C T I O N

W I T N E S S   T O
T H E   S A C R E D

WHY AM I WRITING ABOUT MY SPIRITUAL JOURNEY? WHAT IMPELS me to do this? Forty years of close association with Krishnaji have left their imprint on my life. From the moment I met him to the present time, I feel I have been a witness to something untouched and pure, beyond the narrow chaos of everyday human life. It is this vision that I have held in my heart as infinitely precious.

I learnt much and unlearnt equally. I sat "at the feet of the master," talked with him, shared my problems, and worked with him in the Foundation (KFI). It all had a profound influence in shaping my life and the many decisive turns it took. What gives me a reason to write is an earnest wish to share with readers the events, insights, and conversations with Krishnaji, and the manner in which they helped me face life's conflicts, and led me to begin my inward pilgrimage.

I abstained from writing all these years, but my friends urged me to pen down some of my experiences, as they may be of interest to others. Each of us has our own individualized context in which the drama of life is played out. However, my writings dwell upon those poignant moments in life that we all share as human beings—anguish and loneliness, joy and pleasure, and most of all the deep desire to explore the many unanswered questions of life.

Looking back at my past from a distance of time, I seem to obtain a deeper understanding of the conversations and communications I had with Krishnaji. At difficult periods and situations in my life, I received a kind of guidance or help from him, which would throw light on the state of my mind at that moment. It is a strange thing to say that he did give help, for he took one by the hand only to a point. It was never *"Do this"* or *"Don't do that."* As he said once, *"I can tell you that there is a lovely garden beyond the hill. I can hold your hand, but you have to walk, and climb the hill."* So he often pointed out what was happening to me and the mist of confusion cleared a little, yet ultimately whatever action followed or did not follow rested on my level of understanding, insight, and perseverance. It was not a traditional *guru-shishya* (teacher-student) relationship in which the guru guides the pupil at every step. He did not lay out a path for one to follow.

One of the reasons for his lack of authority may be that he was a sensitive teacher who took the student only so far as her conditioning and capacity to understand would allow her to progress. For perhaps he knew that beyond that point the pupil would only blindly follow without understanding. The point I want to stress is that I was learning, not obeying; I was seeing and listening to everything around with attention and care. In that state, one's sensitivity became heightened, the mind became subtler, there was a quickening of perception, and eventually an understanding was born. However, whenever I obeyed or followed without authentic insight or comprehension, then I paid the price of it, which was continued ignorance and conflict.

It is fascinating to see how the kind of guidance Krishnaji gave me changed through the various stages of my life. For instance, in the initial years I used to go to him with personal problems, and he responded with affection and care. And I grew to depend on this care and kindness. Later, this changed completely. We would not discuss problems or issues but only the state of my mind, my self-created impediments to perception. I had to work it out. He would say, *"Don't be personal or emotional; see what is actually happening."* *"Wake up,"* he would say; *"time is running out."* He appeared very harsh in his admonitions, but it was only born out of his concern and urgency for one's predicament.

What is it that drew thousands of seekers like myself to Krishnaji? His presence seemed to cast forth a flow of compassion, energy, and radiance that transmitted a sense of wonder, a feeling that one was in the presence of something sacred. Because I have been a witness to this presence during my many years with him, I can say with certainty that there is something like the "sacred" in life and in the all-pervading universe. If I had not met him and felt that presence, I may never have felt that palpable vibrancy, compassion, and immense emptiness of silence. It would not have been tangible through his books, or through descriptions of it in the Upanishads or in the sayings of the Buddha. From time to time, from epoch to epoch, when a truly religious teacher lives and speaks, he communicates this sacredness, in response to the times and the needs of human consciousness. Krishnaji was such a teacher in the twentieth century, and his way of liberation was a new song.

Krishnaji seemed to hold the presence of a mind that was in a timeless state. I was a witness many times to an intelligence that did not emerge from memory or thought but revealed itself through illuminating insights. We had come upon the sacred in dialogues with him, in interviews, conversations, and small group discussions. In some of the public talks, one could feel an extraordinary intensity—an ethereal, intangible feeling of benediction. It has been captured in some of the videos. One could see it on his face, feel it in the atmosphere and in the seriousness of communication. I witnessed this personally one morning at Vasanta Vihar in Madras when I went up to his room to give a message. As I entered the room I saw him sitting there in a lotus position, eyes closed, with his back straight against the wall. His face was glowing with ecstasy. There was such joy and radiance on his face that I stood rooted to the spot and then slipped away quietly. How can one describe the beauty of that face?

Having thus been a witness to the sacred through the presence of Krishnaji, I have often wondered how a seeker in the next century would respond when reading Krishnaji's books or listening and viewing his audio and videotapes. Would Krishnaji's physical absence make any difference to the profundity and beauty of what he communicated? Would the sacred be felt without his presence? People who in the years to come feel drawn to the teaching may want to know more about the person who was Krishnaji. Written records like mine, though subjective, may provide through various anecdotes a sense of his living presence.

In the following pages I speak of my observations and experiences, which I have recorded for years in my diaries. I have traced the path of my life's events and have included various insights I have gained on these events, through the years. Therefore, the narrative continually interprets the past from my present understanding of life. To give coherence to the varied mosaic of my experiences, I have summarized them under different sections. I now set out to trace the path of my journey to its beginnings.

PHOTOGRAPHS

*Krishnamurti with
Sunanda Patwardhan
(right) and Radha Burnier
(left), Vasanta Vihar,
circa 1984.*

*Sunanda Patwardhan,
when she met
Krishnamurti for
the first time in 1947
at Madras.*

*Sunanda Patwardhan's par-
ents, Vishwanatha Iyer and
Rajalakshmi Iyer.*

Sunanda Patwardhan at Pune, 1982. Photo by Evelyne Blau

Krishnamurti at a question-and-answer meeting at Vasanta Vihar, Madras circa 1980.

Krishnamurti speaking at Vasanta Vihar,
Madras, circa 1980.

A small group discussion at Vasanta Vihar,
Madras. Left to right, Radha Burnier,
Krishnamurti, Dr. Sudarshan,
Pupul Jayakar, and Pandit Jagganath.

Sunanda, circa 1986.

Sunanda Patwardhan and Pupul Jayakar on the verandah of Vasanta Vihar, Madras, circa 1980.

Pama Patwardhan, Sunanda Patwardhan, and Theo Lilliefelt (Trustee of KFA) in California, 1976.

Krishnamurti chanting Sanskrit verses with G. Narayan and Sunanda Patwardhan in Bombay 1980. Photo by Asit Chandmal

Krishnamurti and some members of his three foundations at Rishi Valley, 1980. Photo by Asit Chandmal.

Radha Burnier lighting the lamp at the opening of the Krishnamurti Center, Pune, November 1998. Left to right: Radha Burnier, Sunanda Patwardhan, Satish Inamdar, and R. R. Upasani.

Sunanda at the Krishnamurti talks, Madras, circa 1975.

Sunanda Patwardhan in front of the Sahyadri Study Centre, Pune, November 1998.

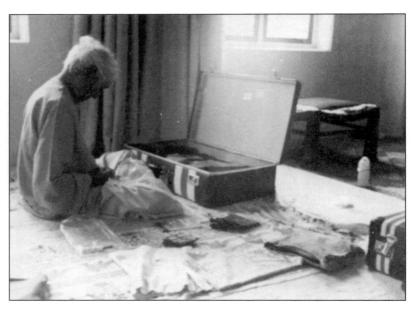

Krishnamurti packing his suitcases to depart Vasanta Vihar, 1986.

MY SPIRITUAL AWAKENING

THE FIRST ENCOUNTER

MY SPIRITUAL AWAKENING STARTED FIFTY YEARS AGO. IN September 1947, Krishnaji had come to India, and his public talks and dialogues were to be held in Madras. At that time I was living in Bangalore with my parents and had to go to Madras to receive my degree. My family encouraged me to attend Krishnaji's talks while at Madras. Krishnaji's host at that time was Mr. Madhavachari, who was a close friend of my maternal grandfather. I visited Mr. Madhavachari, who received me warmly and treated me as a member of his household. He then introduced me to Krishnaji.

The urge to find truth or meaning to life, the impulse to search for perfection, lies in each human being, but few of us are aware of it or even seek it. It seemed as though this urge to inquire into the meaning of existence had lain dormant in my consciousness. Some of us awaken to this seed of inquiry through a search for meaning or through the practice of various kinds of meditation; others nourish it by seeking a life of peace and sanity. Yet others come to it through their pain and suffering. The seed also bursts into life in the presence of a great religious teacher. It was so with me. Something within me responded deeply and immediately to Krishnaji on our first meeting.

When we met for the first time, I was swept away by my affection and his response to me. He was so beautiful, full of affection and joyousness. His face was extraordinary, a chiseled perfection with eyes that seemed to look into the far beyond. His presence to me was that of an enlightened and radiant being. I felt protected and secure in this presence. The bond that I felt for him was to be a life-long one.

I don't think I differentiated between the teacher and the teaching. Krishnaji had said so often that *the teacher is not important; use him like a telephone, but live the teaching.* I can understand that he tried to imply one should not be dependent or be a follower, and that the teaching is perfect and it is that which must help one to feel one's way. Despite that, I must confess that Krishnaji as a person meant a lot to me. The extraordinary experiences that I had in his presence have had a deep and indescribable impact on me.

My first meeting with Krishnaji was unforgettable. To recapture and recollect what happened half a century ago is rather difficult, but from the very first conversation and in the many that followed, I got the feeling that Krishnaji saw in me a religious "something." He told me so, and I responded to him from that source. He talked to me, gently opening out new horizons, perhaps to test the strength and depth of my feelings. I was not analytical or even aware of the depth of his words at that time.

When I look back upon my first meeting and the following months of my association with him, I see my destiny beginning to unfold. It brought me to him at a very early age, when I was not too young and yet still innocent of the world outside, having been brought up in a protected brahmanical family. It seemed as if an already woven pattern were revealing itself, and a new direction in my life began. Meeting and being with him was the first decisive turning point.

In 1947, I was like many other young persons, full of plans and ambitions to study law and jurisprudence, try for the civil service, and so on. At the age of twenty-one, with the fullness of adulthood, the path of my future seemed to be clearly laid out. However, all that changed dramatically after my meeting him.

How did this deep and immediate change of mind occur? What acted as a catalyst? Today with hindsight, I can discern some factors that may have been responsible for my spontaneous response to the call of the sacred. I would attribute my immediate response to Krishnaji to my family and its Theosophical legacy and to my marriage.

THE EARLY YEARS
OF MY LIFE

ONE'S BIRTH AND CIRCUMSTANCES PLAY AN IMPORTANT ROLE IN shaping one's life. To be born human is itself a gift, and growing up in a family that was concerned with the sacred was an added advantage.

I grew up in a simple South Indian brahmanical milieu, along with my two brothers, Krishnamurthy and Premanand. We grew up amidst much affection and care. My father, Vishwanatha Iyer, came from a traditional middle-class family from Thanjavur, in Tamil Nadu. He was well educated and worked in the judiciary. My mother, Rajalakshmi Iyer, belonged to an aristocratic and progressive family. Her father, M. N. Ramaswami Iyer, was a distinguished person and a devoted follower of Dr. Annie Besant.[1] He often hosted her and other Theosophists in his home.

My family was a conservative one. We lived an austere and simple life, and my parents brought us up with a sense of morality and integrity. They had a great deal of warmth and affection and shared it in abundance with our friends and relatives. Although few religious rites or rituals were observed in our home, festivals like Navaratri, Dipavali, and Pongal were celebrated with great happiness.

Both my parents were members of the Theosophical movement, which deeply influenced their belief in an austere and moral way of life. Humanity to them was one large family undivided by race, caste or religion. Truth to them was universal, beyond the narrow confines of rites and rituals demanded by any religious system. My parents had long been followers of the world teacher, Krishnamurti. Brought up as I was in such an ambience, the religious persona of Krishnaji may have already been a part of my unconscious.

THE FIRST
TURNING POINT

THE IMMEDIATE AND APPARENT OUTCOME OF MY FIRST MEET-ings with Krishnaji was the giving up all my earlier plans of further study. There was a deep, unknown force that seemed to compel me to follow him and the teaching.

In 1947, when I first met Krishnaji, he said to me, *"You are like a frog in the well. You have not traveled or seen anything beyond Madras and South India. Take a year off, come to Pune, Delhi, and other places where K will be giving talks, meet people, observe, and then you will find out what you want to do."* The meeting with Krishnaji was a "chance" or an act of destiny, but my decision to go with him, giving up a career, was voluntary. In a real sense, there was no choice. I had to leave home to find out what life held in store for me.

In those days it was not the accepted conduct for a girl of my circumstances to leave home before marriage. However, my parents felt that I was unduly blessed to have been chosen by such a one as Krishnamurti, and with a full heart they bade me go forth into a destiny initiated by him. I moved out of the cocoon of my home, deciding not to continue higher studies but instead to travel and expand my horizons as Krishnaji had suggested. Krishnaji gave me a generous gift of three-hundred rupees and a cashmere shawl of his when I first left home. It was like starting on a pilgrimage.

I traveled to Delhi and Poona (now spelt Pune) with Krishnaji. At Delhi he made it possible for me to meet people from different walks of life—the literati, the wealthy and the politically powerful, the Gandhians and government bureaucrats. As it was the first time I had moved out of the confines of my home, I was a little overawed by what I saw and the people I met. I was exposed to the ways of the *haut ton* as well as the heated political discourses of the Socialists. It was a completely new world, and I watched and learnt in silent fascination.

It was during my visit to Pune that I met Pama H. Patwardhan, whom I married two years later, in 1949. In Pune, the Patwardhan family were Krishnaji's hosts, and they organized and arranged his public talks and small group discussions. Pama's elder brothers, Raoji and Achyutji, were very close to Krishnaji, who had a great regard for them. Both of them were very articulate and participated in many dialogues with Krishnaji. Achyutji's association with Krishnaji dated back to 1928 to the historical event at the Ommen camp.

The Patwardhans came from Ahmednagar and belonged to an illus-trious and cultured family. The family was large, composed of six broth-ers and a sister. They had a rather austere and serious view of life. It was a strange coincidence that they too had a Theosophical legacy. The father was an ardent Theosophist and was deeply devoted to Dr. Annie Besant. The family was heavily involved in the political and social movements of the time. Many of the members of the family, including Pamaji, took part in the Independence movement and were imprisoned during the free-dom struggle. Raoji and Achyutji, the two older brothers, were national heroes. They had spent the best part of their youth fighting for the free-dom of India. Achyutji was a founder member of the Socialist party and one of the Socialist leaders who were active in the Quit India movement. He went underground for five years to escape arrest by the British.

Soon after India attained independence, Achyutji and Raoji were offered positions of power, which they refused. They had a far wider perspective about the human predicament and a larger vision for the country. They held that mere social reform and planned development would not bring about an egalitarian or a just society. They saw the truth of Krishnaji's fundamental message that unless there is a radical transformation in human consciousness, conflict and sorrow will continue to shadow human life.

After my marriage, I became a part of the group around Krishnaji. Among the members of the group who spent their lifetimes with Krishnaji were Raoji, Achyutji, Pupulji,[2] Nandini,[3] Balasundaram,[4] and Narayan.[5]

MARRIAGE AND THE UNFOLDING OF RELATIONSHIPS

WHEN I TOLD KRISHNAJI THAT PAMAJI AND I WERE GETTING married, he neither approved nor disapproved, but he did give his blessings. I knew that in those early years he looked upon marriage as a disaster, especially for women in India. He regarded it as a hindrance to a religious way of life as one gets enmeshed in it. I was, however, fortunate in my marriage, as Pamaji shared my reverence for Krishnaji and responded deeply to his teaching.

Krishnaji was to change his views on marriage in later years, after watching young people being attracted to the teaching and then moving away from it. Many youths who had joined the Foundation eventually got back into the stream of life. He felt that sex, with all its attractions, overwhelmed young people when they were in their twenties and thirties. He felt that they should experience sex, marriage, and begin a family so that by the time they were forty years of age, they could be ready to ask more fundamental questions about life.

I found after my marriage that my relatives were not very demonstrative, and the expression of emotion was regarded as unbecoming and looked upon as a sign of weakness. I told Krishnaji about this. He said, *"You want to be loved and fulfilled, Sunanda, but it can never happen; it is like trying to pour water into a bucket with a hole. However, if you start loving and caring for people, and become sensitive to others—not only to people but also to all things from the earth—then self-concern becomes less. And that strange thing called love can then come."*

I used to talk to Krishnaji about sex and marriage and their place in the religious way of life. I had felt that they were somehow contradictory. One day in Rishi Valley, we were in Krishnaji's room, in the old guest-house. We were standing before a window, quietly looking at a canopy of trees nearby and the hills beyond. He turned to me and said, *"Sunanda, man has always associated passion only with sex. Do you see that stray dog down there on the road? Do you feel passion for it? Do you feel passion for that village woman walking over there, carrying a heavy load on her head? Do you feel passion for a flower? For a beggar? If you don't feel intensely for all that, then sex becomes a shoddy little affair."*

Krishnaji did not advocate celibacy as a necessary preparation for one who has chosen to walk the path, as he felt it often led to an unnatural suppression. At the same time, he also pointed out the ill effects of promiscuous sexual relations. As I understood it, he seemed to say that sex had to find its place in the wider context of life. There had to be an understanding of love and passion. To attain this understanding, one had to go beyond the frontiers of thought and image in relationship. Only then would one understand the proper place of sex in life.

Understanding begins in the way we live our daily life and in the harmony created between body, mind, and emotion. He seemed to say the body should be looked after properly, with the right food, right exercise, and so on. The brain too should be alert, questioning and observing the world within and without; then sexual demands find their own level. *"Can one live intensely with great depth and awareness, live with wonder? To care for another, to look after a plant? This is a movement away from self-concern. When self-concern becomes less, then desire and its demands are less. You will then see that there comes a harmony of living in which sex finds its right place."*

Krishnaji pointed out that just as knowledge had its right place, sex too had its right place in life. Everything in life had its proper place. He said, *"If my father and mother or your father and mother did not sleep together, neither I nor you would be here. It is natural. But what has gone wrong is that human beings have made sexual pleasure into something all-encompassing, exclusive, and ugly."* He seemed to feel that it was essential to understand the role of thought in relation to sex. Thought remembers a pleasurable sexual experience and makes images, dreams, and fantasies about it. It wants to repeat the experience and get more and more of it. He held that one had to understand that it was thought that had made sex into an enormous problem.

No wonder, he said, that the ancients advised, *"Control thought, then you control desire."* Thought, desire, and control are interrelated. He felt control was not the answer, for that which is suppressed comes back with reinforced energy. *"Neither control nor indulgence can give the right perspective."* He held that it was only in realizing what love is that one understood the right place of sex. *"Where there is love, you can do no wrong."* One has to understand how he defined love. Love, according to him, is not jealousy, envy, or attachment. Love means to have passion. Passion is an intense feeling that can express itself not only between a man and a woman but also in one's profession or work. When our concern with the self becomes less, then passion extends beyond to cover the whole of the earth. It is like a vast field of belonging, feeling responsibility for people and for the things of the earth. I could understand from all this that sexual life is such an infinitesimally small part of one's life, and that all relationships could be beautiful and sacred where there is love.

If there is no love in daily relationships, life becomes a wasteland. To love and to be loved is a fundamental need of ours. When one refers to the word *love*, it generally conjures up images of romantic pictures, of sexual pleasures. However, I am talking of the little gestures of affection, concern, and care that bring a certain fragrance to our daily lives. In our homes, it is sensitivity to the other—be it wife, husband, parent, children, helpers in the kitchen or garden, or friends—that makes all the difference between neglect or indifference and appreciation. To be aware of and acknowledge the many little things that one receives from another, not taking the other for granted—all this is part of affection. The sexual aspect of a man/woman relationship is only a part of one's total life. If one gives attention to what Krishnaji has pointed out about love—the right place of sex, the function of thought and stimulation, the need to be sensitive, and a larger commitment beyond self-fulfillment—then perhaps people will have a fresh look at sexual desire and its role.

Sexual desire is also related to loneliness, and understanding its roots frees one. We observe that people are becoming increasingly self-centered, concerned with their own pleasure and satisfaction, so that there is little left for giving. Moreover, in this pursuit we isolate ourselves, alienating ourselves from other people, from nature, and then inevitably loneliness becomes the biggest problem. Though most of us try to escape this feeling in many ways, we all know that deep down that sense of isolation does not disappear. An inward fullness born of a different dimension alone can remedy this.

L I V I N G   I N
C O N T R A D I C T I O N S

FROM 1952 TO 1960, I WORKED AS KRISHNAJI'S PROFESSIONAL stenographer, looking after his correspondence, making notes of his talks and question-and-answer sessions, and typing them out. I used to do this in Vasanta Vihar, Rishi Valley, and Rajghat. So each year, for a couple of months or more, I traveled with him and spent the rest of the year in my home at Pune. That was the pattern of my life at this time.

Looking back, I realize now there were sharp contradictions in my life during these years. When I was with Krishnaji, my mind was charged with energy and was alive and vibrant with a keenness to absorb the subtle nuances of the teaching. There were many serious people who would come to meet him, and the ensuing conversations and dialogues kept one continually alert and attentive. I was observing and learning, and there was much work to do. Life in Pune, on the other hand, for the rest of the year was that of a householder. It was a different ethos. It was a hectic life filled with friends, relatives, and social activities. My home was open and we welcomed our many friends who often came to visit and stay with us. Entertaining, cooking, gardening, and going to the club kept me busy. I was also a member of some social welfare organizations. However, this was a life vastly different from the religious one I led with Krishnaji.

By the standards of the day, my life as a householder would be considered full and enriching. But problems gathered like dark clouds at the approach of a storm. I had several miscarriages during the first ten years of my marriage, leaving in their wake extreme anxiety and psychological trauma. They had to be dealt with. Although I appeared to live with zest and energy, dissatisfaction was brewing beneath the surface. Leading two different lives took its natural toll, for the one seemed to have little relationship with the other. Being with Krishnaji, working for hours with the teaching, meeting a fantastic variety of people, engaging in dialogues and serious conversations—all this was so different from the householder's life in Pune.

In addition, when I came home from my trips with Krishnaji, restlessness came upon me; adjustments and compromises had to be made. It was like continuously switching gears. The two lives ran on parallel lines—two languages, two atmospheres, and two separate parts of myself. The two parts did not harmonize or coalesce into a whole. Inwardly deep contradictions were tearing me into disparate halves.

ANOTHER
TURNING POINT

SOMETHING DEEPLY FUNDAMENTAL BEGAN TO TAKE ROOT IN MY mind. After my constantly listening to the teaching and discussions and transcribing them, Krishnaji's words began to fill my mind. I realized that instead of authentic insights, I was often repeating his words and ways of expression. I had become stale and reached a dead end spiritually. I felt that I had to get away, be on my own, and find out what was happening to me. I seemed to have lost my sense of direction, and frustration was creeping in. It was a perfect time to stand on one's feet and start walking by oneself. By coincidence, from 1960 onwards, tape recorders began to be used to record his talks, so that my role as stenographer ended quite naturally.

Why did I not see all this confusion clearly at that time? I feel, perhaps, that I had come into all this when I was too young. Drawn to the teaching and the teacher, I plunged into the religious path without having experienced the full gamut of life. I had thought I was almost on the threshold of the path when I first met Krishnaji, but obviously I had to go through the fire of life and get burnt by its experiences before attaining some depth and authenticity as an integrated individual.

I told Krishnaji that I had to do something on my own. Some part of me felt suppressed, and I needed an outlet, a safe house. He seemed to understand this. My life was at a crossroads, and I did not know what I wanted. Questions of "Where am I going? Where is my life leading me?" crowded my mind and left me confused.

A SEARCH FOR IDENTITY

WHEN KRISHNAJI WAS LEAVING INDIA, I ASKED HIM WHETHER HE would give a few of us who were present something by way of a message or statement to ponder over during his absence. *"Do you seriously mean it?"* he asked. We nodded in response. To one, he said, *"Don't be ambitious"*; to another *"Have an even keel"*; and to me, *"Be yourself."*

So I started with questions, "What am I? Who am I? Am I a bundle of thoughts, emotions, desires, or am I something more than that? What is this 'myself'? What is this entity composed of? What is this 'me' to which I am holding on so tenaciously?" As self-inquiry began, questions arose about the nature of the self, and the very process again triggered greater inquiry. It released a new kind of energy.

Another occasion when Krishnaji helped me inquire into the self was in Bombay. After watching me being quiet in the small-group discussions, Krishnaji said to me, *"Why have you been quiet? Are you afraid of speaking? Are you shy? What is it? Do you want to be like Rao, Achyut, and Pupul? Don't. Sunanda, be yourself."*

It was an insightful statement. I was able to perceive some truths about myself. I realized that I had developed a diffidence to speak in front of people who I thought were far above me in their intellect. I felt the other speakers in the dialogue had powerful personalities and were articulate in their exposition of what they wanted to convey, and I felt inadequate. The feeling that I was a "nobody" seemed to have taken root at these meetings. After Krishnaji's talk with me, I tried to take part in the dialogues without being self-conscious.

The most difficult thing is to be oneself and to have self-worth. One feels like a "nobody" or "nothing much" or "just a housewife," only in comparison with another and the judgment of social peers; otherwise each one has an uniqueness that can express itself when it is left unhindered by comparison, made by oneself or by others. It is not difficult to see this process operating in oneself. To judge or evaluate oneself in relation to another's achievements or one's own expectations implies a subtle conformity and comparison to some set parameters. Behind these comparisons seems to lie an un-understood frustration with oneself, a deep dissatisfaction, for hidden within lies a strong desire to achieve, to be recognized, a yearning for rewards and successes.

How often we long for something we do not have or are not able to get. It may be a longing for affection, for material comfort, luxury, or any other thing in the world. It is in such states of reflection and perception that one sees the fleeting nature of fulfillment and self-expression. Another aspect of this inadequacy is that one seeks appreciation from others for what one is or for what one has achieved. If I want any kind of appreciation, I see I can never be a free person.

The process of wanting is so subtle. If, for instance, my article appears in a prestigious journal, I feel elated. If it is not accepted, then there is frustration. To be dependent on the appreciation of another for your self-worth is a never-ending pursuit of illusion. When you see the truth of this, the hold of the achieving mind loosens. You are then able to acknowledge this part of yourself and not fight it. Then there is no conflict within. You accept yourself with all your personality traits, capacities, tendencies and inadequacies. You wear no mask. This is a natural state of being. It is certainly a beautiful thing to live that way, for in it there is simplicity and vulnerability. Many things can happen when one is not fighting oneself. There is a letting go, a naturalness in being related to people without images.

I can see this clearly today. However, at that time Krishnaji's words did not have the same impact.

THE CONTINUING SEARCH FOR FULFILLMENT

MY LIFE CONTINUED TO BE FILLED WITH CONFLICT. I FELT family life itself held no true attraction for me, for marriage had not fulfilled its promise of a child. There was a great emptiness in my heart and a deep void in my life. I had three miscarriages in the 1950s. I often confided to Krishnaji my disappointment about these losses. In those years, as I have narrated, he used to help me face my problems, opening my eyes, heart and mind to what was happening to myself. It is amazing to me how extremely confident I was then about my ability to see things as they were. After one of the miscarriages, he asked me, *"What is happening to you?"* I said, "It is all right, Krishnaji. I have accepted it. I am not destined to be a mother. I know that nothing more could be done." I was sure that I had understood my losses, sorrowed for them, and gone beyond disappointment.

Krishnaji unfolded to me the way of "going through" an experience so that no residue was left. He said, "*You have to allow this thing to come out. See what it has done to you. Watch it. Watch yourself when going out for a walk. What happens when you see a lovely child holding its mother's hand and walking along the road? When you open a book with photographs of lovely children, what is your response? Is there a sorrow, is there envy, do you feel like bursting into tears, is there a sense of denial, of having missed out on something? Watch it. Does that extraordinary feeling of affection and tenderness come out? Or do you feel, 'I wish I had a child'?*"

On many occasions, he would ask me to probe and find out for myself the depth of the feeling of denial and open it out. "*When you so observe, everything in relation to that denial speaks to you. At the end of it, what happens? When and how will it end? You may not consciously know it, but it has told its story, revealed itself, and you have listened. Then, whether you have a child or not becomes totally irrelevant. You have come out of it, whole. It is a flowering of the deep feeling of denial. Do not allow the intellect to act. The intellect is a very inadequate instrument to understand life.*"

This process of understanding seems to be one of listening without any resistance or rationalization. In listening, the depth of one's feeling rises up to the surface. In the beginning, one may not like to acknowledge what is happening to oneself. We often think, "I don't like this feeling in me." But allowing these feelings to expose themselves is the wiping away of the pain and longing. The wiping away removes the sense and feeling of denial.

Looking at the years that followed, I can say I did not miss having a child born to me. In my life there has always been a sense of a much larger family, not born of blood ties but born of a natural relatedness to young people in the family and outside.

Again, I feel that things happen to one with a purpose. If I had had a child of my own, perhaps my capacity for detachment would have been sorely tested. I have yet to see any mother who has no attachment, and I do not know whether I would have passed that supreme test of detachment. It appears now that not having a child was really a fortunate thing for me; it became easier to accept and understand loneliness and solitude. As in marriage, one can stagnate in one's family life too, one can be held by it. As the flowing river moves over the obstacles it encounters, so also one's life goes on. We wade through psychological potholes and puddles and take shelter at wayside inns, and with attention we can continue to move on with a heightened wakefulness. What seems to be required is a diligent mind to see the ways of attachment and its impact on our lives.

The years 1959 to 1969 were a period when I was completely on my own, exploring new areas of interest and learning new skills. This was a decade devoted to academic pursuits. I completed my doctoral studies in sociology with distinction, and taught at the University of Pune until 1969. In 1968 I spent six months in the Advanced Centre of Sociology in the Delhi School of Economics and published my first book, *The Change among India's Harijans*.

The new life brought its own challenges and tensions. Academic life meant hard work, fuelled by a burning desire to do well. I started with a great deal of diffidence, as it had been fourteen years since my undergraduate studies. There was my family life with its complicated webs of relationships. All this with my teaching load created a lot of strain. I was not aware of the intensity of my work and the colossal energy that went into fulfilling my varied roles until it began to take a toll of my health. The first signs of physical illness began in 1968. The "worldly" virus also crept into my mind, insidiously. The sense of achievement, success, and praise boosted my sense of self. How much the "I" fed itself on all this, and I was enjoying all of it, of course!

I remember well a conversation with Krishnaji that roused me from this euphoric slumber. I had gone to tell him of my many successes in the academic world. He kept quiet for a while and then said, "*Sunanda, don't be vain. Do you know that as you came into the room, the feeling of vanity was there in the room? Be watchful.*" He then added, "*All right, you have your Ph.D. now, and then what?*" I had no answer to give him, for I had none to give. However, it made me pause and observe the movements of my life and thoughts. I was indeed fortunate to have received this advice at the appropriate time. I had become vain and self-important with my little "successes" and achievements. There is nothing wrong in excellence, by itself. One has to be excellent in whatever one does. But worldliness and strengthening of the ego seem to accompany these achievements, and that is the problem.

LOOKING INTO ONESELF: THE PROCESS OF OBSERVATION

KRISHNAJI'S WORDS TO ME, *"BE WATCHFUL,"* WERE SIMPLE AND direct. I seemed clearly to understand what it meant to observe or watch oneself. During the early years he had asked me to write down each thought and feeling, pleasant or unpleasant, as I observed them. By watching a thought/feeling to its end, one had a sense of the meditative process. These were my first lessons in meditation. During this process one's private thoughts, intentions, aspirations, and hidden motivations come upon the surface. In addition, one begins to know oneself. The initial exercise of coming to know oneself starts with watching one's thoughts, feelings, and experiences; and as one observes, they seem to open up, revealing their contours, textures, and colors. Hidden as well as conscious desires, loneliness, and sorrow paint their picture. A process of awareness begins, and one becomes a witness to how thoughts and emotions arise and fall. One sees how swiftly thought moves, changes, and flits from one thing to another, sometimes logically but mostly randomly, chattering and churning. Awareness also brings into focus the way the "me" acts as the controller or director, trying to change "what is" to "what could be" or "what should be." Thus, there comes a stage when one is familiar with much of the content of consciousness.

During this process of continued observation, an interesting thing takes place. The map of consciousness opens out. But however intensive and wide may be my knowledge about the psychological facts about myself, it does not necessarily release me from my everyday feelings and fears. For instance, when I look at my anxiety, I wonder why I continue to get anxious when I am fully aware of the causes of it. Self-knowing then seems to be a continuous process of observing the arising of thoughts, their movements, and the interval between thoughts. In this interval, there is a steady state of non-movement.

On the one hand, there is this subtle and sustained watching of thought; at the same time there seems to be a futility in doing this. Krishnaji puts this process in proper perspective. *"Merely to pursue, analyze and be aware of any particular thought is utterly useless, if one has not understood or observed the interval between two thoughts.*" I feel it is necessary, as part of meditation, to observe the interval between thoughts. If one so observes the interval, then one notices that the fleeting, weightless, flimsy thoughts fade away. For in that space of silence, no judgment, comparison, or controlling is taking place. Until watching one's thoughts is accompanied by observing the interval between thoughts, one's awareness does not attain depth. In that interval of space, a feeling of infinite space can be actually experienced, if there is no desire to prolong its duration or pursue it. "*This means,*" he said, "*really infinite self-knowledge. In that interval a new and different feeling can come into being.*"

When one sees the horizontal flow of thought/feeling, one observes how the very watching opens out the roots of that thought/feeling. Then one touches a deeper level of consciousness. It is the "thought-free" witness to the space between thoughts that adds a new dimension to experiencing. As this space extends inwardly, sometimes breaking the borders of thought, there is silence. That silence is a very important aspect of meditative potentiality. That silence/space becomes the ground for the fertility of insight.

Krishnaji also talked of a state that exists beyond conditioned consciousness, beyond the comparable. To quote, "*There is definitely a stage that is not comparable, to be chosen, to be wished for. It is to be oneself, this oneself which is stripped of all the rubbish of civilization. It is. Love has no choice, no wish. That is the key of life.*"

I am still wondering what is this state that is stripped of "all the rubbish of civilization." To use the word "all" is forbidding. One can be aware of the extent to which the blockages in one's mind have disappeared. So asking questions like "Have I eliminated all blockages?" is a self-defeating question. For instance, has the anxiety or ambition that was present in me completely disappeared? Yes and no. It seems to appear in different contexts. So what do I do? I can only observe it and watch it dissolve for that moment.

This whole process of awareness appears to me as a dynamic movement, each observation adding depth, strength, and vitality. Without awareness, there is no beginning. Without coming upon original insights, the inner journey lacks strength and support. The journey itself has no end point but is itself the only way of living.

I CONTINUED TO BE A MEMBER OF THE FOUNDATION. EACH YEAR I attended the talks in Bombay and spent some time in Rishi Valley or Rajghat or Vasanta Vihar with Krishnaji. I was not part of the happenings in the Foundation. I was out in the wider world, working and living on my own steam, going through various enriching experiences. The feeling of relatedness with Krishnaji was very much there, but it was different. He never asked me to give up anything that I was doing. I had to go through life in the outside world without leaning on him. It was the first break from my dependency on him.

The years 1964 to 1969 were also a time when Krishnaji's attention was greatly engaged in the West. He was dissatisfied with the events and some of the people in the Indian Foundation. There was an impercepti-ble but definite withdrawal of the earlier warmth in his relationships. These were also the culminating years of conflict and the break in his relationship with D. Rajagopal.[6] New people had gathered around Krishnaji and taken charge of his financial and other interests, including the legal battle against Rajagopal. They arranged for his tour schedules, talks and dialogues, and the publication of his works.

This was the time when Brockwood Park came into existence. The KFT (Krishnamurti Foundation Trust, UK) and KFA (Krishnamurti Foundation of America) were formed during this period, and the link with the earlier organization, KWINC (Krishnamurti Writings Incorporated), was severed. There was also a psychological distance between the Indian Foundation and the newly formed foundations abroad. Responding to Krishnaji's dissatisfaction with us all, some of us, including Raoji, Achyutji, and me, resigned from the Foundation for New Education, which was the earlier name of the Indian Foundation. This name was later changed to the Krishnamurti Foundation India.

However, by 1969, there was a change in his relationship to the Indian Foundation. Pupul Jayakar became the president when Mrs. Kitty Shiva Rao[7] gave up that responsibility. I was again nominated to be a member in 1969. I remember Krishnaji arriving in Delhi in 1969, on his usual annual visit. When he saw all of us gathered at the airport in Delhi to receive him (Achyutji, Pupulji, Nandini, some others, and myself), earnestly and simply he said, "*You have not abandoned me!*" It was his way of saying "*Pax.*" He was back to his normal self with a fullness and warmth of affection towards all of us.

FACING SORROW

DURING KRISHNAJI'S 1969 VISIT TO INDIA, KITTY SHIVA RAO'S husband was seriously ill, and she had therefore resigned from the presidency of the Foundation. Krishnaji was often with her during those distressing times. I was present once when he advised Kitty on how to deal with her sorrow. She was deeply attached to her husband, was terrified of his dying, and could not conceive of a life without him. Krishnaji comforted her in his own way and yet dispassionately told her, *"You are very nervous about the passing away of your husband. Learn to live from today as though he were already dead. Otherwise it will be too late."*

Though his words seemed stark, they offered an insight that could be liberating, if one could do it. He had so often told me to be psychologically independent of my husband, family members, and others. This would mean psychologically inviting the death of the person whom you love, inviting detachment, much before the event takes place. But very few can do it. One can see the stark truth of what he says, but it has to happen actually and not as something that we intellectually acknowledge as true. That detachment can come when we accept death as part of life and are prepared to go through the agony of loneliness and solitude. His message is for each one of us, young and old, to live in a different way, psychologically.

A PERSONAL RECOLLECTION

THE INCIDENT WITH KITTY SHIVA RAO BROUGHT TO MY MIND AN occasion when Krishnaji had responded to another individual's suffering with great compassion and helped him face the crisis directly. This incident occurred even before I was born. My grandfather, M. N. Ramaswami Aiyar, had lost three of his daughters, aged between twenty and thirty years, within a span of fifteen days. It was a terrible tragedy. On hearing about the dreadful crisis, Krishnaji had written a letter, from which I quote:

2123 N. Beachwood Drive
Hollywood, California
February 13, 1935

My very dear Ramaswami Aiyar,
When I read your letter, I was really shocked by the news you have
written to me. I cannot possibly imagine that such a thing could happen
to you in such a short time. It must have been in every way a perfect
torture to you and to your wife. I remember them all so well, quite clearly,
and I can't imagine that they have passed away.

You know, Sir, I really feel for you about this, and it would be absurd
for me to give you any comfort because in such moments of crisis one does
not want comfort, the suffering is so intense and so acute that consolation
seems such a tawdry affair. But if one has the capacity to maintain that
suffering intelligently, and not discard it, not seek substitution, not run
away from it, but really dwell with it intelligently, and with full integrity
and awareness, I think one will find that there takes place an understanding which gives an inner joy to life. I wish I were there to talk to you both.
Writing letters from this distance seems so casual, but you know, I hope,
that all my sympathy and affection are with you both.

You know, Sir, when one is in this stage of utter collapse and misery,
one wants to find an immediate way of alleviation from all this agony.
And the danger of it is the very impatient desire helps one to find a way
out, but that way is not the true way. So, if I may suggest it, and this
is what happened to me, I assure you, with regard to my brother too, there
should be intelligent patience of continual inquiry, not acceptance of a
remedy, which one finds fatally easy.

It is like this: One never rejects joy; it is so strong, so vibrant, so alive,
so creative that one never questions it, discards it, runs away from it;
it consumes one and carries one in its movement. In that moment of great
happiness there is no question of wanting to get rid of it, or wanting to
find out the cause of joy; one lives in it. Now, in the same way, if I may
suggest, do the same thing with sorrow. Naturally, when one escapes from
it or one seeks a remedy in the innumerable beliefs, or in people, the
fullness or richness of sorrow is diminished; and the man who knows how
to suffer greatly with intelligence, not with acceptance or resignation,
knows the real ecstasy of living.

You may for the moment feel that I am not giving you any help, but *if you would kindly think over it and not be impatient with what I am saying, you will see that there is substance, a reality to what I am saying. A remedy is an end, whereas this richness of understanding is a continual movement; therefore, in that, there are never moments of agony.*

J.K.

This letter was written more than sixty years ago. It has a simple lucidity and abounding affection. It gives us a glimpse of how Krishnaji helped people to cope with profound sorrow that comes with the death of beloved ones.

Krishnaji always spoke about sorrow during his series of public talks in Madras, and it invariably touched me very deeply. The audience unfailingly responded to him at such times with a penetrating silence and receptivity. I would like to describe the atmosphere of one such talk that took place in Vasanta Vihar. Krishnaji was sitting on a platform giving a talk under a canopy of old trees. The sun was just setting in the west and threw light and shadow on the delicate branches hanging down from the ancient trees. On that day, he was talking about the sorrow of man. I felt that Krishnaji's voice was gentle with infinite compassion as he described the river of sorrow, which is only too familiar to all of us. I felt as though each one, in that vast gathering of five thousand people, saw what he said reflected in their life. Each one had his or her own genre of suffering, going through it, accepting it, living with it, and never being able to end it, not having the clarity and strength to tear out the roots of suffering. When Krishnaji talked of human suffering, the whole gathering seemed to be experiencing that vast sorrow of humankind, and each was able to associate his or her own particular suffering with that of the human collective.

IS THERE A WAY TO END THIS SORROW?

KRISHNAJI FELT THAT HUMANITY FROM THE BEGINNING OF TIME must have asked itself if there was something more than this everlasting cycle of conflict and suffering interlaced with fleeting moments of joy. It seems as though the urge to find the meaning of existence lies embedded in all our consciousness. In each one of us there seems to be a continuous search to solve the problems of fear, desire, conflict, and frustration that we face every day. It is these problems that make us inquire and reflect on the predicament that is our existence.

To find a way to end sorrow has been an eternal quest of the ancients in India; they have over millennia inquired if there was something beyond the narrow limits of a time-bound existence, something timeless that could not be measured by man. *"The seed of that inquiry,"* Krishnaji states, *"is still with us. This seed that has been planted in man, in his brain, for millions and millions of years and has never had the right soil, the right light to grow; nothing. Therefore, it is still there. Is it possible for that seed to grow and flower, multiply, and cover the earth?"* [Madras, Dec. 22, 1979]

Krishnaji felt that there was something deeply sacred about the Indian spiritual tradition. The sacred, he often said, is not something to be known or achieved but a search that is necessary for anyone who is intent on crossing the boundaries of thought. However, he felt we had lost this sense of the sacred. He expressed this in a conversation with a group of us in Rajghat. He asked, *"What is happening to the culture of this country, to the Indian mind? Why is it deteriorating? Is it tradition, the weight of it, the authority of the Vedas, the gurus, the British rule, the brief period of freedom? Is it family authority? Are all these factors responsible for the deterioration? Let me put it differently. Look at it* [tradition] *from an ancient point of view: an Indian mind stretched, reached, and sought out the Brahman, the eternal; what has happened to it?"*

Later, he said, *"There has been a disuse of this ancient brain. It was supposed to have worked towards the Highest. That must have been an extraordinary brain. That brain, not the material brain but the brain that is cultivated, have you lost it? On the other hand, have you become specialists, philosophers, Theosophists, neo-Theosophists, anything but That? That ancient mind had done it, worked at it. Have you, the present company, lost it? Or is it* [still] *there to be touched, to be tapped, used to function, flow?"*

He then asked, *"Where is the fountain of the future? Why is there no one who will carry this on? Is it because the Indian mind translates everything? India will connect all this that we are talking about with the tradition here, and the West will deny all this, and there will be greater division."*

Towards the end of the conversation, he said, *"What I am trying to get at is, this country has had this extraordinary brain working* [in ancient times.] *Today, would you let that* [ancient] *brain, that mind, operate? By that brain* [I mean] *the sense of unhindered real inquiry. I am using that word 'inquiry' as a feeling of movement, moving, that is probing, constantly moving, never stopping. Such a mind, then, has a seriousness behind it in its inquiry.*"

I have seen the surging of this seed of inquiry in the spirit of our times. In observing various spiritual movements and the growing importance of meditation in the last two or three decades, it is obvious that the seed is expressing its presence in many ways. Loneliness, conflict, insecurity, wanting to be loved—all these and many other factors push the seed of inquiry into life, breaking through the layers of patterned consciousness.

The impulse to search for the sacred lies within each human being. Krishnaji had pointed out in many ways that the sacred must touch one. There was no "how" to it, and yet we have to move in that direction without wanting to get at something.

INQUIRY IN OUR DAILY LIFE: A PATH TO THE SACRED

CAN ONE LIVE A DAILY LIFE IN SPECIFIC WAYS THAT HELP TO strengthen inquiry? Though Krishnaji never openly advocated a *sadhana*, or practice, I will say from my personal experience that he did expect one to live in a way conducive to a religious life. I feel the first step towards this is to lead a life that is not divided by contradictions and dualities. A purity and honesty in thought, word, and action help to make the mind integrated and enable one to become receptive to the sacred. Krishnaji used to point out that it was very important to keep the brain sharp, the mind alert, and the body clean, and not to misuse one's senses or overindulge in pleasures. There are some specific practices that he spoke about—a disciplined life; the practice of yoga, meditation, and vegetarianism; and an inner austerity in one's life.

One learnt a lot from just observing him and seeing how disciplined he was. He used to practice yoga and *pranayama* (yogic breathing exercises) regularly in the morning, and every evening he went out for a brisk walk. He never missed this routine unless he was ill. He ate what he felt was right for the body. He once said that he never had any appetite or desire for food but ate what was recommended.

He was very particular that the body remain sensitive. *"Only then,"* he said, *"can it be a proper instrument to receive a different kind of energy."* He would tell people not to put their hands on the stair rail, for it was full of dust, and to wash their hands. The body, he felt, must be kept clean.

Inward quietness, he said, was a way of heightening sensitivity. All the senses were awakened when one was sitting quietly. Doing this every day deepened this state. He did not say to practice this at a fixed time each day. He felt each one should do it according to the rhythm of his or her daily life. If I felt like doing it before going to bed or upon waking up, it was all right for me. Each one has to find out what helps him or her. One does all this to bring about a ground of order. Quietness does not come merely by sitting at a place at a particular time day after day; it is a quality of a mind that can be still naturally. It then becomes a renewing process. Meditating, sitting quietly, watching the movement of thought, going out for walks and being alive to the spectacular beauty of nature, all help the mind to be steady. About walking, he often said, *"Don't chatter; walk alone, tasting the deep poise of solitude."*

He talked of order in daily life, both inwardly and outwardly. According to him, order was not something that was arrived at by imposing a pattern of discipline on oneself. He felt any effort from the "self" did not lead to real order. This did not, however, mean that there were no "ground rules." He laid utmost stress on diligence, which he felt created its own ways of harmony. A discipline was then born that gave rise to an order that was natural and not rigorously forced on oneself.

And what did he say, for instance, about virtue and chastity? With Krishnaji, one could never say that he gave the same advice to everyone. To some like me, he advocated austerity and simplicity. I learnt from him what simplicity with dignity meant. To one young girl, not married, he would advise her not to have premarital or casual sex, whereas he might be tolerant with another who was promiscuous. I once questioned him about this double standard. I understood him to say that a person who leads a sexually permissive life would pay the price for it, would become coarse and insensitive. He was often compassionate to the so-called sinner and often said, *"Haven't you heard the saying that a sinner is nearer to the gods?"* He seemed to feel that a self-righteous person would find it more difficult to change because his ego and self-image are very strong.

In his public talks, he did not categorically talk about these values, but he did so in his personal conversations. I, for one, knew that in the wider context and long vision of seeking transformation of consciousness, austerity, diligence, inner balance, and an inward honesty were important. Anyone who looks for codes of behavior will find them implied in Krishnaji's talks, his actions, and his life. These values are not spelt out as patterns and prescriptions, nor insisted upon. Krishnaji's public silence on these issues did not mean they were not necessary. In his communications to me and to some others whom I know, he had clearly spoken about his views on this. A person who is in search of freedom, of a holistic way of life, has to come to terms with right behavior in the light of his or her own understanding and purpose. Yet we see that flowering of goodness is not just a by-product of ethical and moral injunctions. For love, beauty, goodness or virtue to be, we have to go far beyond ethics and values to a state where the "self" has ceased to be. This urge for transformation is a movement towards unselfishness. It is like a spark that lights up consciousness.

Y E A R S   I N   D E L H I :
1 9 6 9 / 1 9 7 5

IN 1969, PAMAJI HAD BECOME THE EXECUTIVE DIRECTOR OF Orient Longman Publishing House, a very distinguished firm of publishers. We left Pune for Delhi, not knowing whether we would return. I had given up my teaching job and bidden adieu to academic life. Delhi was a totally different political, intellectual, and cultural milieu. A new life, full of unknown challenges with all its mysteries and opportunities, had opened.

E X P E R I E N C I N G   S I L E N C E

IT HAS BEEN MY DESTINY THAT AT APPROPRIATE TIMES, IN different contexts of my life, a re-emphasis of my life's direction towards the sacred came from Krishnaji. Soon after we came to live in Delhi, he said something deeply profound and meaningful: *"You have sharpened your intellect. It is capable of analysis, clear thinking. That's enough. Now turn to the other direction, the unexplored part, an explosion of silence in the mind."* Then he further said, *"Enter into a movement about which you don't know anything. Experiencing silence, that is necessary for humanity."* He seemed to indicate that the next direction of my learning lay in the exploration of silence.

The "experiencing" of silence, he seemed to imply, was the gateway to a new mind, and meditation was the path towards this silence. One knows states of "silence," as in expanded space, a being in silence, but "an explosion of silence" is something I cannot comprehend, even intellectually. One can conjure up images or delude oneself that one is in that state, but what Krishnaji said seems to be something much more than just a steady state of silence. Such statements of his, I have always felt, have only to be listened to, to be held in one's consciousness like a jewel, then to be left alone.

This timely suggestion impelled me to put my psychological clock in order. He had revealed the supreme importance of a creative silence. I tried to pull myself out of the mire of a chattering, occupied mind, as I saw it was a blockage. It helped me to sit a little more lightly on the everyday events and problems. This seemed to be a way of gathering oneself from time to time, and observing whether one has moved away from the source of renewal. A flowing river meets obstructions but flows on.

A blade of grass bends with a storm but straightens itself again. Once a seed of awakening has been sown, it does not die. I may cover it up with inattention, allow myself to be smothered or carried away by driving ambitions and desires and family involvements, but the seed is there, alive and dormant. I have always been interested in a vision of the "other," and a state of mind that is not fragmented but whole. My mind sets right the course for itself by a process of watchfulness, cleansing, and being receptive to any "intimations of immortality."

LOOKING AT THE MAP OF LIFE

KRISHNAJI HAD ONCE ASKED ME TO GO THROUGH AN EXERCISE on self-observation, a comprehensive perception of my life at one glance. Could I look at my life as I would a map? He asked me to try this out: *"Take a notebook and write down the story of your life, an unfolding of your personal history, like a map. Let there be rivers, mountains, and craters—everything. Try to trace the whole of your life—the various tensions and conflicts, the body's reaction and the mind's reaction to them, and so on. Do not hide anything. Put down everything that has happened to you, big or small, significant or otherwise, but do not go into details. The outline and the contours of your existence must be clearly seen. Then the totality of it is revealed to itself."*

I sat down and traced out the course of my life. After I had finished, I showed him what I had written. He glanced through it and said, *"Do you see what has happened? You started early in life with the search for truth, a religious flow. That was the little river, like the beginning of a living stream, the source."* Then he pointed out that I moved along and got married. Marriage became a puddle; in it were involved pleasure, security, dependence, and all that went with marriage. Somehow the river continued to flow and did not dry up, but it was thin like a rivulet instead of a gushing stream. *"Now,"* he said, *"look at the other factors—drives and desires that have created puddles, like ambition, the pursuit of success. Look at the whole map, not a bit here, not a bit there, but feel the totality of the whole map of Sunanda's life (it is not you) impersonally, objectively, all of a piece.*" I saw the interwoven patterns made by the conflicts, tensions and competition, all part of the aggressive thread of the ever-present ego with its drive. Unless I was very careful, the whole movement of the "me" would have again weakened the gathering momentum of the river. Krishnaji said, "*Such a meditation or looking is a vast movement in linearity and verticality, of space and time.*"

Observing the map of life with Krishnaji made me aware of my self-created obstacles to understanding. The awareness brought with it energy to overcome some of the blocks and flow with grace. From time to time, during difficult periods I have done a reading of the map of my life, to help me chart my directions clearly. Krishnaji used the metaphor of a subterranean stream, flowing, meeting obstacles, and then moving forward. The reading of the map with attention helped the stream loosen the hard stones of conditioning, enabling new insights and perceptions.

MEDITATING ON KRISHNAJI'S TEACHING

KRISHNAJI HAD OFTEN STATED DURING HIS LIFE THAT THE teaching such as the one that came through his body would not recur for some hundred years to come. He once said to me, "*I am leaving a precious jewel in all your hands. The teaching is a jewel. There is not likely to be another teaching like this for a long time.*"

I recall a meeting with Krishnaji where Narayan and I were present in his room. He asked each of us to say what we thought indicated the essence of the teaching. Narayan said, "You are the world and the world is you," and I remarked, "The observer is the observed."

Krishnaji later told me to go into the depths of the statement I quoted and to let it speak to me. He said one could learn to listen to the thoughts that arise and ask the most fundamental questions like: Who is the observer and what is the observed? What is the nature of the observed? Is there a holistic perception where there is no division between the observer and the observed?

This kind of reflection, he felt, helped one to understand the "self" through its manifested expressions and its hidden roots. One has to be very honest in this journey, stay with one's perception, and not delude oneself. Approximations to the states described by Krishnaji can be misleading. One has to move in this perceptive process with complete integrity. Thus, this process of meditation begins by taking any significant, sutraic, or cryptic statement of Krishnaji's, and pondering over it, probing into it, and living with it, taking its obvious meanings to subtler levels of perception.

There are many sutraic statements of Krishnaji on which one can reflect and observe the actual movements of thought initiated by these statements. In understanding one statement deeply and fully, one can get a glimpse of the truth behind it and experience a state of quietness. At such moments one gets a new insight, and some light is thrown on the nature of consciousness.

Here are a few statements of Krishnaji's that lend themselves to this form of meditation, in my opinion:

The content of consciousness is consciousness.
Thought is fear.
To be is to be related.
Hurt is the essence of the self.
Look without the movement of thought.
The ending of sorrow is the beginning of wisdom.
Where you are, the other is not.

INSIGHTS ON THE PATH: A MYSTICAL COMMUNICATION

EVEN INDIVIDUALS WHO HAVE DEVOTED THEIR LIVES TO THE quest for the sacred often lose their focus and need corroboration of their direction. A strange, esoteric event took place once during Krishnaji's visit to India. I am speaking now about a meeting between a Jain *sadhu* (holy person) and Krishnaji, with Achyutji and I as silent and fascinated witnesses. The *sadhu* told Krishnaji, "Sir, for fourteen years now, I have devoted myself to meditation, yet I am not able to get into *samadhi*. I have been practicing meditation, *dhyana*, but I have not been able to go to the depths of it. Can I do this? Will you be able to tell me what my impediments are?"

Krishnaji asked him to describe the kinds of meditative practices he had been following. After listening to him, he said, "Do you *realize that you are still acquiring? Open your fist. There is nothing to acquire.*"

For some minutes, the *sadhu* was silent. He then got up and prostrated himself before Krishnaji, who then asked him to stay on for some more time. After a while, the sadhu said, "Sir, I want to ask you one more question. Is it the impact of your personality that has given me this [experience]? Is *this* due to your *gurukripa* [grace of the guru]?"

Krishnaji replied, "*I knew you would ask this question. That is why I asked you to stay on for some more time. This is not something to acquire but to give up. Release your fist. Leave everything.*" He paused for a moment and said, "*Is it the* [new] *mind that is asking that question? Or is it the mind before you experienced 'this' that is full of questions? You have been caught up in it again. I took you out of it, but you have gone back to it. If you stand firmly on that and let go everything, 'it' will come. 'It' will come, not because you want it, but 'it' will come. Have you understood what I am asking?*"

The *sadhu* prostrated himself again before Krishnaji, sat down and said, "I don't need to go anywhere else." Krishnaji then said to him, "*The 'other' is out of time, and we live in time. And we want to bring timeless into time. I have told you all this, but it is not mine.*"

Unknowable are the nonverbal experiences and mysterious are the ways by which a teacher communicates them. What I understood from this conversation is that transformations in oneself could take place in the presence of an enlightened person if one was open and vulnerable to the teaching.

THE PUBLICATIONS IN KFI

IN DELHI, ANOTHER ROAD WAS OPENING OUT FOR ME. I FOUND myself taking up responsibility for certain essential functions in the KFI. It meant editing and publishing Krishnaji's works in India and publishing Indian-language editions of the works. Part of my function was to liaise between the KFT and KFA about publication matters. Personally, it gave me scope to be in touch with the teaching and to act with a sense of responsibility. I began working with Pupulji. She generally endorsed the policies and dealt with matters between the foundations. Those years were happy and fruitful ones, and my working relationship with Pupulji was fulfilling. She was an important person in Delhi, holding many positions in the government and acting as the cultural *chargé d'affaires* for India. She was a close friend of Indira Gandhi, who was prime minister then. In spite of Pupulji's many engagements, we found time to work together in her house, sitting on the beautiful spacious lawns. There was mutual respect and affection, and this continued throughout her life.

It was around that time that the Foundation decided to begin publishing a quarterly bulletin on behalf of KFI, to announce Krishnaji's travel program and speaking schedule. Shiva Rao was requested to take up this work, and I was to assist him. Very soon after, however, he fell ill, and I took up the editorship of the KFI bulletin; I held that position until Krishnaji's passing in 1986.

That was the beginning of a new relationship with Krishnaji. In the wondrous fifties, I could do no wrong. I never had any apprehensions, and there was a certain easy communication. I was much appreciated and perhaps fussed about a little, not only by Krishnaji, but also by some other members of the Foundation. There was no organizational element either in my work or in my relationships. The sixties were for me a movement towards independent arenas of interest. Activities were not centered on the Foundation. Krishnaji continued to be affectionate and caring, and yet my contact with him was less.

With this new assignment, however, changes inevitably came. There were now two levels to my relationship: one was a personal relationship, and the other was responsibility to the organization, of which Krishnaji was the *de facto* head. These two threads were subtly different and difficult to weave into coherent patterns. In taking up official Foundation work, I had stepped into a situation where it was no longer just a personal relationship; other actors and relationships came into play, making it a network of conflicting judgments and appraisals. This was not so dramatic while I was in Delhi, but the potential for future complexities was already there, hidden, as yet unnoticed by me.

T R A D I T I O N   A N D
R E V O L U T I O N

IT WAS ABOUT THIS TIME THAT I HAD A FIRST GLIMPSE THAT organizational work was not going to be easy. I will narrate an incident about the beginning of *Tradition and Revolution*, a book of dialogues with Krishnaji, as an illustration of difficulties to come. These dialogues took place in Shiva Rao's house at Lodi Estate in Delhi. As early as 1952, I learnt typing and shorthand to be of service to Krishnaji. I had done this work for Krishnaji out of my affection and devotion to him. I continued to attend to his correspondence whenever it was necessary over the years. I also took down notes of the lunch- and breakfast-table conversations and the impromptu small-group discussions that took place spontaneously.

It so happened one evening that Krishnaji did not go for his usual walk. Pupulji, Nandini, and I were with him in his room. He turned to Pupulji and asked her, *"Why don't you question me from various traditional points of view?"* Thus began a series of dialogues on questioning the mind and the traditional approaches. Each day a certain topic or question was probed. It was thus that the book *Tradition and Revolution* was born. I believe it is one of the first books of dialogues to be published in India. It was also the first publication of the KFI using material that had been gathered solely in India. This set a trend for further dialogues for questioning the nature of the self and inquiring into it from different perspectives. I had taken down the dialogues in shorthand, transcribed them, and typed them out. Krishnaji was quite excited and wanted these dialogues to continue in Rajghat, Rishi Valley, Vasanta Vihar, and Bombay. The book was very well received; for example, when Pamaji and I met Dr. David Bohm[8] at Ojai, he told us that *Tradition and Revolution* was most useful for his understanding of the teaching.

I am writing in retrospect about the history of this book to illustrate how small differences could become complex in an organizational framework. When the dialogues were ready for publication, Pupulji and I signed our names as editors. The KFT and KFA at that time had raised some doubts about the authenticity of these dialogues and wanted to remove the editors' names. Later, when they came to know from Krishnaji that I had taken down the dialogues in shorthand, they had to accept my work as authentic.

Because of this incident, there arose some differences between the Indian and British foundations in terms of publication rights. These rights were originally held by the KFT, who were reluctant to relinquish their hold, which explained their resistance to our independent publication. The Indian production of the book thus set a new trend: each foundation from this time onwards commenced publications independently.

MY LIFE IN DELHI

MY LIFE IN DELHI REVOLVED ON TWO AXES, ONE THE "K" ambience, and the other the outside world. From the time Pamaji and I started living in Delhi until the time we left, Krishnaji's statements and observations helped me keep the religious dimension alive.

Delhi had its distinctive ambience. Krishnaji met a fascinating variety of people, including politicians, diplomats, bureaucrats, sociologists, journalists, *sadhus*, and others. Some of them were invited for lunches and dinners at Pupulji's house and some for seminars. Many public figures sought individual interviews. These conversations were very private. They included talking over a problem or sitting quietly in nonverbal communication. Whatever the form of contact was, a feeling of communion seemed ever-present.

We had a beautiful house in Golf Links, which was an aesthetically planned residential area. Twenty-five years ago, Delhi was a good place to stay; there was no polluting smog hanging over the city, and the environs of New Delhi were clean and beautiful. It was an impressively laid-out Lutyen's city, with elegant avenues of trees and landscaped gardens. Our house in Golf Links was very near the Lodi Gardens, where we used to go for long walks. Krishnaji often joined us in our evening walks when he was in Delhi.

Pamaji was now the executive director of Orient Longman Publishing House. He was one of the partners of the firm. Delhi was the headquarters, but he traveled often to its offices in Bombay, Calcutta, Madras, Hyderabad, and Bangalore. We interacted with people mostly from academia and the literati, professors, journalists, diplomats, and others who were keen to have their writings published. It was a life that was undoubtedly stimulating, and Delhi offered a plethora of cultural activities, too—plays, concerts, exhibitions, and so on.

With the publishing office of KFI at my home, it was easy for me to attend to the publications and have the freedom to participate in other activities without a feeling of pressure. I had now come into close contact with people in the educational and philanthropic fields, and I sat on the boards of a few organizations like Bal Bhavan and the Red Cross.

When Krishnaji was in Delhi, he used to come to our home for lunch. He met different groups of people—Gandhians, social activists, architects and others—at our home. Altogether Delhi was a place of political power and patronage, each faction jockeying and manipulating to get into positions of power. Even personal relationships seemed to fall prey to these political machinations.

At this time I felt no contradictions between my personal life and my religious one. Why? Perhaps it was my focus on K's work that kept the direction alive. The work revealed the ephemeral nature of positions and friendships, and helped me to retain perspective. One did get caught in the whirlpool of activities; it would have required extreme awareness not to be sucked into the stream of immediacy. Our life did not take psychological root. That is why, when the time came for us to leave Delhi, there was no anxiety or insecurity.

ANOTHER
TURNING POINT

BY 1973/1974, SERIOUS DIFFERENCES CAME UP BETWEEN THE partners and the board of Orient Longman over financial policies. Pamaji and his family had only a minority stake in the company, and they decided to dispense with it. In September 1975, we bade goodbye to Delhi and to Pamaji's professional life. It was a very crucial and critical phase in our life. I was nearing fifty and Pamaji was fifty-eight. His giving up a successful profession with all its perquisites made this a difficult time. He received a few offers from other businesses but decided not to take up a professional job. Unseen, changes had also taken place within him. He had come closer to Krishnaji during our stay in Delhi. He used to visit Krishnaji at Shiva Rao's and Pupulji's place, and an acquaintance was growing. Pamaji felt that all his life he had been pushed by circumstances and family influences and that he had no control over many situations. He felt it was time that he found out where his real interests lay instead of just taking up another professional assignment. Earlier, Krishnaji had already cautioned him, *"Pamaji, you have been under the influence of your two elder brothers. Shake it off. Do not be influenced by my words, too. Find out what you love to do."*

Our life was at a crossroads. Pamaji and I discussed whether we could devote our life to what we truly wanted to do and live from our earnings. Could we change our lifestyle? I welcomed it. So the decision was final: we would leave Delhi not knowing what we were going to do.

I talked to Krishnaji about our plans during his 1974/1975 winter visit. He told me, *"What are you doing here in this place? You have a sharp brahmanical brain, but you have traveled enough on this route. The time has come to put an end to this. There is nothing new to be learnt anymore on this path. Once you have learnt, mastered something, give it up. Intellect is not the instrument of perception. It is a good tool only if you have right perception."* He urged me to leave Delhi, saying, *"This is a mad place. It is a place of power, patronage, and of much excitement. You will get lost if you continue to stay here."* I said to him, "Yes Krishnaji, we are leaving, we will go back to Pune." He disagreed emphatically, *"No, Sunanda, don't go back to Pune. The Patwardhan family is too well known. You know too many people there. You will be lost there. Go to the south. Be anonymous."*

So that was how we chose Bangalore as our new place of residence. K's parting statement to me in particular at that time of leaving Delhi was to change my destiny. For, if I had gone back to Pune, it was very unlikely that Madras and Vasanta Vihar would have played a major part in my life. His advice urging me to go south instead of to Pune was almost like a premonition.

TRANSITION

NINETEEN SEVENTY-FIVE WAS THE DREADED YEAR WHEN Indira Gandhi[9] imposed a state of emergency on the nation. She canceled all civil liberties and imprisoned leaders from the opposition political parties. Krishnaji did not come to India, owing to the declaration of emergency. I wrote to him that we were going to the south, to Bangalore, where my family had lived for many years. In his letter dated September 24, 1975 from Brockwood Park, he wrote, *"Your decision to get away from the north will bring about a non-fragmented life."*

How perceptive he was! My life in Delhi was not all that it should have been. Pamaji had a myocardial infarction, and there was the stress of coping with it along with his business pressures. My body was not too healthy and was weakening under repeated attacks of rheumatoid arthritis. But for Krishnaji's care, my illness could have severely handicapped me forever. My mind was churning and revolving around many things, without a focus, nor was there a deepening of inwardness.

Two questions began a refrain in my troubled mind: How does one live with a religious quality in the marketplace of life with all its conflicts and confusions? What is that something within oneself that can help one get through the conflict and turmoil of self-involvement without being drowned? I am still seeking answers to these questions.

INTERLUDE : 1975/1976

LIFE IN BANGALORE

BY THE MIDDLE OF SEPTEMBER 1975, WE WERE WELL SETTLED IN our apartment in Bangalore. My parents were also living with us. The first few months were idyllic. We had no work, no pressures, nothing in particular to do. Pamaji had been made a member of the Foundation, and I was looking after the publications and editing the bulletin from my home. It was a total change from the earlier hectic pace of living in Delhi. We did not seem to miss it at all. We did not know many people except a few relatives of mine. It was a time of leisure, going for walks in the Lal Bagh or Cubbon parks. It was like floating easily on the waters without knowing in which direction one was moving.

However, destiny had laid its own path for us to walk on. It was not mine alone but Pamaji's too, for we were to become an integral part of an unfolding scenario that began with a letter from Krishnaji dated December 14, 1975.

> *My dear Sunanda,*
> *...I feel it is important that you should come to Ojai for the scientists' conference. Do think about this seriously....*
> *J.K.*

Again, he wrote, on February 16, 1976, from Ojai:

> *Dear Sunanda,*
> *...I hope you have decided and found the means to come to Ojai. I do urge you to come. As I have not heard from you, I am writing this again. Do come a week or so before the conference begins so we can talk over things together, not only about the conference but also about things in general in India.*
> *You have to make Vasanta Vihar a real center. It is your responsibility. You have to create it and work for it....*
> *J.K.*

It was the first hint I had from Krishnaji that he intended to entrust the care of Vasanta Vihar to Pamaji and myself. Vasanta Vihar was an essential element of Krishnaji's consciousness, for it was here that he came into his own after leaving the Theosophical Society. It was a safe haven for him and became the first established center of the Indian Foundation.

OJAI: A SENSE OF THINGS TO COME

I RECEIVED AN INVITATION FROM ERNA LILLIEFELT[10] TO VISIT Ojai, which said, "We expect you and your husband to stay at Arya Vihara during your visit here. Krishnaji wishes you to come a week before the scientists' conference if it is possible."

Thus began the new journey and our first visit to the United States and Ojai. We arrived in Los Angeles, and Mary Zimbalist[11] drove us to her elegant house at Malibu. We were given a warm welcome. Mary took us to our room and told us, a little apologetically, that it was rather small for the two of us but that she had no other room to put us in. Krishnaji overheard her saying this and said, *"Maria, it is all right. Pamaji will sleep in the hall."*

Krishnaji gave me a great deal of affection and attention. He was "cooking" me, to use his familiar expression for preparing and training individuals for a particular responsibility. It was to be the responsibility of taking care of Vasanta Vihar.

He spoke of many things to me and stressed the importance of building Vasanta Vihar into a living spiritual center. I cannot recall everything he said, but some of it remains very vivid even now. Some of these words to me were like a benediction: *"I want to give you so much, pour into you so that something may happen. You have to do it. Stay here for a long time. Let us see what happens. You have to talk and live for this."* Though I was totally in the dark about what needed to be done, his asking gave me the courage to accept. He said, *"Sunanda, be simple. It is not you that is doing it."*

We left Malibu on March 18, 1976 for Ojai. Krishnaji drove the Mercedes belonging to Mary Zimbalist. He drove for an hour on the Pacific Coast Highway with the deep blue ocean on the left and the mountains to the right. The drive was unforgettable, as the entire landscape seemed to come alive in Krishnaji's presence.

Krishnaji showed us round Arya Vihara. He told us that the room we used had been Nitya's room. Krishnaji reminisced a lot about Nitya, about the times they had spent together in the early twenties.

The scientists' conference began a week after our arrival. It was attended by eminent economists like John Platter and others from the Club of Rome, and by professors of sciences, humanities, social sciences, philosophy, literature, and other fields. The persons with whom I came into close contact were Professor David Bohm, Dr. David Shainberg,[12] Professor John Briggs,[13] Dr. René Weber, Dr. E. C. G. Sudarshan,[14] and Alan Kishbaugh.

At the conference, I was put to a test. Krishnaji asked me to speak after Professor David Bohm gave his inaugural speech. I was totally unprepared for this and literally quivered with nervousness. I started saying, "Krishnaji, how can I? These people are all great scientists. I am nothing. I cannot do it." Then he said, *"Just talk. Do not be nervous. I am there."* Therefore, I did as he suggested. Even today, I don't know what I said or did. The people we met were intelligent, friendly, and articulate. It was my first taste of interacting with people of such high intellectual caliber. I was deeply enriched by the experience, and many that I met were to become familiar faces in the years that followed.

During our stay at Ojai, Krishnaji was to address a psychiatrists' meeting in New York, organized by Dr. David Shainberg. Krishnaji requested Dr. Shainberg to invite Pamaji and me to the conference. He arranged our trip to New York, hosted us, and graciously gave us his room. He was a friendly and hospitable person. He said to me with great humor, teasing me, "Sunanda, what do you know of psychiatry? Why does K want you to attend?" I said, "It is simple, David. He knows I don't know anything. So he wants me to observe eminent psychiatrists like yourself and understand how you dialogue and interact." It was rather a tense conference. Krishnaji questioned the efficacy of analysis and pointed out that putting fragments together still did not make a whole. It was a difficult thing to accept that thought and analysis had no part in healing a patient. Some were perturbed and felt deprived of the very tools they had so long used for dealing with mentally sick patients.

Our trip to Ojai and New York were thus wonderful opportunities for observing and learning. Soon after we returned to Bangalore, we moved to Vasanta Vihar.

VASANTA VIHAR:
1976/1986

NEW BEGINNINGS:
REVITALIZING
VASANTA VIHAR

THE PROPERTY OF VASANTA VIHAR WAS NOT AVAILABLE TO Krishnaji and his work between 1968 and 1976, as it was locked up in a legal controversy with Rajagopal. The latter had tried to gain possession of Krishnaji's properties by dubious means. In May 1976, the high court judge initiated a compromise by which the property of Vasanta Vihar was handed over to a new trust called the Krishnamurti Trust Madras (KTM), of which Krishnaji was the trustor for life. The trustees were Radha Burnier,[15] S. Balasundaram, Achyut Patwardhan, myself, and two lawyers from either side. Radha Burnier took charge of the place and was the secretary of the trust. Pamaji was appointed as the secretary of Krishnamurti Foundation India. KFI and KTM jointly carried out all the activities of the Foundation.

I took charge of Vasanta Vihar in July 1976, and together Pamaji and I started to build it up with the help of friends. Unoccupied and uncared for, the place was in a shambles. I remember my first impression of Vasanta Vihar: a wild garden with overgrown grasses over four feet high, and a snake seen moving across the ground, then disappearing ever so swiftly. In the main building the plaster had peeled off the walls, outside and inside. There was no underground drainage or electrical cabling.

From the time Vasanta Vihar was restored to the Foundation, Prema Srinivasan,[16] Padma Santhanam,[17] and Mr. T. S. Santhanam rendered invaluable help and cooperation in transforming it into a hospitable and beautiful place. They had affectionate devotion for Krishnaji and for the work connected with Vasanta Vihar. By December 1976, when Krishnaji came to stay there, accompanied by some members from KFA and KFT, the place was ready to receive them. Talks and discussions, meetings and seminars were held there that year. Vasanta Vihar had come into being as a full-fledged headquarters of the Krishnamurti Foundation India.

My primary function was to keep the place worthy and elegant for Krishnaji's stay so that he was comfortable. Organizing the talks, discussions, question-and-answer meetings, publicity, collection of funds, spreading of the teaching, recording of the talks, making audio and videotapes available for the public, and the maintenance of the property were some of the functions of the secretary.

The publication of K's works was the most important responsibility, as this was central to the spreading of the teaching. Over twenty books and pamphlets were published during the two decades I was there. More than forty translations in several Indian languages—Hindi, Gujarati, Marathi—were completed, and a KFI quarterly bulletin was published. I was the secretary of the publication committee, and Pamaji's expertise in the publication field was of great help to me.

RESPONSIBILITIES AT VASANTA VIHAR

PAMAJI AND I HAD THE TASK OF MAKING VASANTA VIHAR A conducive place for Krishnaji to stay when he came to Madras to give public talks and dialogues. The most significant feature of working there was the special relationship I had with K. He asked me to report on every-thing that was happening, not only in Vasanta Vihar, but also in all the K places in India, and all other Foundation matters. I used to write to him regularly once a fortnight. If I were ever slack, he would remind me immediately of it.

When I look back at all that I did, and was expected to do, I am amazed how I went through such a complex situation for such a long period of time. I can truthfully say it was only because of Krishnaji's affection and understanding that I was able to keep going. But I was not spared the "stick"!

Nineteen seventy-six to 1986 were the years when, for the first time, Vasanta Vihar really came into vibrant existence. It became the active headquarters of the KFI. Krishnaji was very keen that it should grow into a beautiful place and become a religious oasis. I have looked upon my time at Vasanta Vihar as a small corner in the total landscape. It was also a period of contradictory demands, conflicting personalities, and some impossible goals—almost like a kaleidoscope, a varicolored mosaic. Inlaid in it were K's presence, his energy, the insightful dialogues, con-versations, and the various personalities.

Many images float before me. One of the most memorable images I carry with me is of K standing behind the door of his room on the first floor and looking down at the people gathered under the canopy of trees waiting for his talks to begin. Many people would arrive for the talks two to three hours earlier; some would be seated in meditative poses while others talked together or waited silently. Krishnaji would come down for the evening talk, dressed simply and elegantly in the traditional *dhoti* and *kurta*. He would be inwardly far away; he was always like that before a talk. His consciousness seemed to undergo a strange transformation, and he appeared to be different from his normal self. One naturally viewed him with awe and kept a respectful distance from him on all such occasions.

At the other places where his talks were held, someone or other always accompanied him to his seat. Here at Vasanta Vihar he would walk alone to the podium, unaccompanied. I felt this was because he regarded this as his home, as much as it could be home for a person like him who had no permanent abode. His passport address was c/o Vasanta Vihar.

DREAMS FOR VASANTA VIHAR

HOW DID HE LOOK UPON VASANTA VIHAR? HOW DID HE VISUALIZE it to be in the years ahead? What were the activities, functions, and programs to originate from there? He seemed to lay an extraordinary importance on Vasanta Vihar and its function as the center for the dissemination of his teaching. My role and Pamaji's function as secretary of the KFI were integral to the building up of the place.

Krishnaji had given me a check of ten thousand dollars before I left Ojai as the initial amount for the renovation of Vasanta Vihar. He has said many things to me about what a study center should be. During this time, Krishnaji did not specifically use the term "study center" for Vasanta Vihar. Later, it symbolized itself into that, and all the other study centers in Krishnaji's places followed this pattern.

Vasanta Vihar was not like a school. Many times he expressed the wish that it be meant only for adults who were attracted to the path of self-knowledge, particularly to the ways in which Krishnaji had opened the doors of perception. The atmosphere had to be quiet and conducive to a reflective and contemplative life.

In a discussion with him in the car en route to Rishi Valley School from Madras in 1983, I took down the following notes:

"Vasanta Vihar should draw people who have a good brain, a good intellect. They should study the "teaching" thoroughly, soak in it deeply as you would do if you were to study medicine or Buddhism or any other subject. Studying means to go deeply into the subtleties of the words used and their contents and seeing the truths in them in relation to daily life. They should be able to discuss the teaching with specialists in any branch of knowledge, as scholars do. While they are studying, these people should have a spirit of cooperation.

A spirit of cooperation does not mean working together for some purpose, but it means that one is able to share one's discoveries and findings with one another. For instance, I share with you as a friend what I have discovered. You may doubt it, question it, but I am sharing with you the discovery. It is not my discovery; it does not belong to me or anybody. Perception is never personal. Such a sharing is cooperation. But it must not be confession. There are groups in many places that confess to each other, like washing your own dirty linen in public.

And suppose I am a liar; it is the responsibility of you and all the friends who are in Vasanta Vihar. Because we are all interested in the "teaching" and in studying it deeply, and in living it in our daily life, we are responsible to each other for whatever we are. This togetherness among friends who are interested in the discovery of truth in their daily lives, who share a sense of responsibility for each other is the spirit of cooperation. And when everyone who lives in Vasanta Vihar has this spirit of cooperation, that will create an atmosphere in which a newcomer will also flower."

During one of Krishnaji's visits to Madras, he told me a little about the religious way of life: *"Vasanta Vihar is a place where people come only to be a light unto themselves. There is no guru, no authority, no following. The individuals who come here must not only meditate, but also must work with their hands and have leisure to learn so that the mind is not occupied. They should not pick up a novel or read to occupy the mind. Discussions and dialogues are necessary. A person in the group should be able to get up and say, 'This is my problem, I would like to discuss it with you.' They are not to be fed, in the sense of psychological guidance."*

THE QUALITY OF MIND IN A RELIGIOUS PLACE

KRISHNAJI SAID CERTAIN THINGS TO ME WHEN I CAME TO LIVE IN Vasanta Vihar in 1976. These seem extraordinarily important from today's perspective and convey an immense depth of meaning. One thing that I distinctly recall and cherish were his words, *"Sunanda, feel completely at home here. This is your home. Feel safe, happy, but do not take root. Be a guest while you are here. See the beauty of this, being a guest in life and to be able to live that way."* By this I think he meant not to take root in a place nor to be attached to the work, the place, or even to the person or organization of which one was a part. It also meant that one could not seek security in any place.

He seemed to convey two messages. The first was not to be attached to a place and find psychological shelter. One could so easily and unknowingly get used to a place and become attached to it. But how is one not caught in this net of attachment? The second message was that one had to feel a total sense of responsibility for the place and for the work one had undertaken and yet not feel identified with it. Responsibility without identification, he seemed to reveal, was the way of detachment. It is only when one is watchful and observant that this perception and the right direction continue. He used to say, *"Be responsible,"* not only to Vasanta Vihar but to Rishi Valley, Rajghat, Brockwood Park, Ojai, and all the places. "How could this be?" I said to him, "What could I do for other places, living here in Madras?" He pointed out that it was not a matter of doing something: *"It is the feeling of responsibility per se, not merely responsibility for some thing. This feeling is precious."* These statements touched me deeply, and I wanted to feel my way into all this, the concern for teaching, for the place, and for everything that one did. I felt that I must have a sense that "I am responsible," and so wherever I was, I would act with this feeling. This concern for the larger, I felt, would give me the right perspective when working with the particular.

The full import of what Krishnaji had envisaged for Vasanta Vihar revealed itself gradually through the years. He had indicated that to be in charge of one place meant that my consciousness must be full of the place and its demands. While that is necessary and inevitable, it is also essential that I felt equally responsible for the larger, for all the places. I truly understood the import of such a holistic understanding when I had to face the challenges of seeking solutions for other places, and when creating common ground for all the Foundations. It was like saying the earth is ours, for all living creatures, including humanity, and that it is our sacred responsibility to do whatever is necessary to nourish it. This consciousness seemed to bring a wider vision to the work we do in our specific contexts.

Krishnaji gave me a crucial insight regarding the quality and nature of mind necessary to create a religious place. He gave great importance to not being hurt. He said, "*Sunanda, don't be hurt, ever. When you live in a place like Vasanta Vihar and you have to work towards making it into a religious place, hurt has no place, for hurt is the essence of the self.*" One can see clearly that when one has an image of oneself, one feels hurt. This image is the self. Clearly what he was trying to convey that as long as an image exists, hurt is inevitable. If I live with that, as he said, I will be polluting the place. Therefore, the challenge from him and from oneself was to see that one wiped away hurt and, at the same time, was watchful not to be hurt or to hurt another.

Today, after many years, when I see people getting hurt, I see the truth of his words and feel like sharing this with them. One may not be involved in creating a religious place, but hurt does infinite damage to the psyche. I feel there is urgency for each human being to understand the profoundness of not getting hurt in order to live in harmony within and without.

A MONTH AT
VASANTA VIHAR

KRISHNAJI SPENT A MONTH OR MORE EACH YEAR DURING THE decade 1976/1986 at Vasanta Vihar. It was the most eagerly awaited moment of the year both by the Vasanta Vihar residents and the entire city of Madras. His public talks at Vasanta Vihar attracted over five thousand people. Theosophists who attended the annual convention at the Theosophical Society during December of each year would be present in large numbers. With welcoming arches, spruced-up gardens, and the radiance of Krishnaji's presence, Vasanta Vihar seemed the perfect setting for the series of talks, question-and-answer meetings, and discussions.

I would like to outline the images that are with me about Vasanta Vihar during Krishnaji's visit. It will give the reader an idea of how intense each of his visits was. Every winter, during December/January, Vasanta Vihar took on a new look and feel during Krishnaji's stay. He used to give six public talks; this was later reduced to four in order to lessen his strain. There were question-and-answer meetings, seminars, dialogues, and unscheduled informal small-group discussions and conversations. Altogether he had a very heavy schedule; he met many kinds of people, gave interviews, or met them at lunch, where the conversation would go on long after the meal. Some people could go to him directly, for they were like his friends. He met some by previous appointment, and I used to look after all the arrangements for their interviews. In later years, he stopped giving such interviews. Those who were not able to meet with him felt that it was people like us, the hosts, who prevented them from meeting him. I could understand their feelings, but there was no basis for it.

Nearly forty persons—members, friends of the Foundations, and those invited—were guests of the KFI during this period. Hospitality was at its best. Menus were worked out; tables were laden with a variety of Indian dishes to tempt the palate. There were many cultural events to entertain the guests. At least two to three performances by leading musicians were arranged by Premaji, as Krishnaji used to enjoy listening to Karnatic music.

The place was full with people. In the garden, groups of people sat, relaxed, talked or seriously discussed the teaching. They would wait for a glimpse of K when he went out for walks in the evening. Krishnaji did not miss going out for his evening walk, unless he was unwell. Krishnaji walking on the beach with four or five friends, the breeze blowing through his silvery hair, is an indelible image impressed in my mind's eye.

I was naturally busy and responsible to see that everything went off without a hitch. Our friends (and it is impossible to mention every one of them here) helped in different ways. Each one did his or her best for Krishnaji. All had a relationship with him, and this could be clearly seen in their actions and demeanor.

Krishnaji gave that indescribable quality of "otherness" to Vasanta Vihar by his presence each year. The talks were held under the age-old trees, which were a silent witness to his energy, compassion, and insight into life and death. The energy that flowed from the talks seemed to envelop the entire place. A special feature of the talks in Madras was that, because Krishnaji lived there, people could linger in the garden to catch a glimpse of him, or sometimes sit with him on the steps after a talk. So many of them have told me that they personally felt his compassion, and some said they felt a tremendous energy pass from him to them. Krishnaji had once said to me that a self-aware person left an aura behind, and that such presence lasts a long time.

There were some factors that I felt added to the unique ethos that existed at Vasanta Vihar. One was that Krishnaji's presence created an indescribable sense of sanctity. When one was there, one could not help feeling it and responding to it. Then there were the seminars, dialogues, and breakfast- and lunch-table conversations, which were spontaneous acts of inquiry often leading to original insights. In all these discussions, Krishnaji seemed to use the dialogue as the means to both inquiry and insight.

DIALOGUE   AS   A   TOOL
OF   INVESTIGATION

THE LAST FIFTEEN YEARS OF KRISHNAJI'S LIFE MARKED THE RISE of dialogues as a profound means of exploring the nature of reality and truth. There were a variety of dialogues, "gatherings" where a dialogue was held between a small number of people, not more than twenty or so. Then there were formally organized "seminars" not exceeding thirty, with invited participants from home and abroad. Finally, there were the informal but extremely penetrating "table conversations" at breakfast and lunch. Each had its own atmosphere.

In the dialogues, Krishnaji's method of investigation was through inquiry and analysis. It is a paradox that the dialogues started with thought as the tool of investigation, whereas he had so often repeated the statement, "*Analysis is paralysis.*" Why was this so? Many have pointed to this contradiction. It is obviously clear to me that we have only thought as the instrument of investigation to question, probe, and come upon new discoveries, paradigms, and so on. So whatever the area of investigation be, we start with the analytical process and comprehend it. Krishnaji's mind was such that it started, as he said, with not knowing. He then led the investigation with others, watching the flow of the dialogue and analyzing the issue. At some point, an insight would come that thought is an inadequate tool to understand the complexities of the psyche or to investigate into the nature of freedom.

Krishnaji once said to me, "*A dialogue is very important, for it is a form of communication in which questions and answers continue till a question is left without an answer. Thus, the question is suspended between two persons involved in this. It is like a bud with untouched blossoms. If the question is left totally untouched by thought, it then has its own answer because the questioner and the answerer as persons have disappeared. At this stage, the investigation reaches a certain point of intensity and depth, where it acquires a quality which thought can never reach.*" It is at such a time that his statement, "*Thought realizing its own limitation becomes quiet,*" was significant. It was a new insight. He has shown how such a mind, when it is quiet, can use thought in a totally different manner. As I understand it, right perception helps us use thought in its right place.

THE SEMINARS
AND GATHERINGS

THE SEMINARS BEGAN IN 1976 IN MADRAS, AND I WAS RESPONS-
ible for organizing them for over ten years. The small-group discussions
began as early as 1948 in India and continued through the years in
different places, especially in Bombay, Madras, and Varanasi. These have
been published from time to time by the Krishnamurti foundations.

In the seminars, Krishnaji tried to awaken the insight of his listeners
and participants by inquiring into the nature of the human mind. People
attended the seminars from different disciplines and cultural streams;
they included Vedantins and Buddhists, scientists and philosophers,
writers and artists, specialists in computers and seekers of truth. There
were a hundred or so observers who listened to the seminars.

The events were concerned with the investigation of consciousness,
and various issues were explored, such as bondage and freedom,
sorrow, fear, aging, death, loneliness, truth and reality, to name a few.
Issues that formed common ground with philosophy and science had a
dominant place, and these were discussed with eminent physicists,
scientists, and others. These explorations into the nature of the brain,
mind and consciousness, the process of thought and time, the nature of
insight and intelligence, threw new light on the inner process of consciousness and offered glimpses into the sacred and the timeless.

Seminars took place over three days—each issue was confined to
that day, to that period and that moment of insight. It took place in
Krishnaji's presence and had his total attention. He initiated the dialogue
and took up a theme from the various issues raised by the participants.
The dialogue had no premeditated pattern or course. It was a dynamic
movement in inquiry. Therefore, each dialogue was unique to that
context and location. Books and audio and videotapes have frozen them
on paper and tape, but that evanescent quality of a live intelligence operating with precise logic and clear insight cannot be re-created. The act of
inquiry is a continuous movement and cannot be repeated exactly, just as
the flow of a stream is never the same.

In a dialogue, a few people gathered in seriousness posed a searching
question. Not all the people who were present participated. A few
did actively; others listened in attention, watching their responses to

others and in themselves. Krishnaji would start by throwing open the subject and making others ask questions and express their views and ideas. His mind, it seemed, started with not knowing, a state in which there was an absence of views, hypotheses or postulations.

Very often, it appeared that his mind seemed to be moving in a different direction from that of the participants, almost as if it were a separate thought movement. The dialogue moved along parallel lines for a while. Suddenly, somewhere in the middle of the dialogue, this parallel movement came to a stop. The dialogue seemed to take on an immediacy demanding that the participants observe and reflect on the here and now. The atmosphere changed and gathered intensity and energy. There was a surcharged feeling and a sense that the dialogue had taken on a life of its own; it seemed to unfold itself, nourished by the observation and perception of Krishnaji and the participants. The flow gathered momentum as new insights were revealed. The insights did not belong to Krishnaji or to anyone in the group. It was drawn by the energy of inquiry, and its light unraveled the coils of the problem.

On one such occasion, Krishnaji pointed out how a question opens out a dialogue. He said, *"When a person asks the question, instead of answering, when there is no immediate response from the listener, the question begins to open and in the very unfoldment is the answer."* Further he said, *"We never at any time say, 'I don't know.' It is not a conceptual statement to say, 'I don't know,' and wait for something to happen. On the contrary, if one is really in a state of not knowing, what happens?"* He then made a leap and said, *"That may be love. If you are in the state of not knowing, there is love."*

The beauty of these dialogues lay in the evanescence of the dynamic movement. Sometimes, at the end of such a dialogue, a silence would descend, as if the energy lay in fragrant stillness holding each one in thrall, and revealing itself in the stillness. It was a silence that seemed to touch one deeply and change one's consciousness, if only for that moment.

The seminars were stimulating occasions. There were members from KFA and KFT, and the invited participants included a dazzling variety of intellectuals, scientists, religious people, writers, and others. Off and on, there would be a questioning as to whether such seminars were useful, purposeful. At the end of a two- or three-day seminar, Krishnaji would ask me, *"Do you think it was all worth it? Did they understand what we were talking about?* (He always referred to himself in the plural, as "we," never as "I.")

Two years after Krishnaji's passing away, the dialogues were recommenced at Vasanta Vihar under the auspices of the Centre for Continuing Dialogue. I was the convenor. We had five such seminars/dialogues, and four of them have been published under the titles, *Nature of Dialogue, Learning about Consciousness,* and *Dialogue on Death.* I was responsible for organizing and editing them for publication.

Dialogues are undoubtedly essential for inquiry and insight. Very often, they tend to become verbal and deteriorate into sophistry or rhetoric. Most of us don't know how to dialogue or to listen to another. We often make speeches. Each one needs to listen to another, to hold the words instead of bursting out with what one wants to say. On a few occasions when a few minds start investigating with seriousness, the group moves together and we come upon new ideas and understandings. Yet somehow, without Krishnaji, these seminars seemed to lack the vitality and dynamism we experienced before.

GATHERINGS AND CONVERSATIONS: RE-CREATING THE DIALOGUES

I WOULD LIKE TO NARRATE A FEW CONVERSATIONS TO GIVE THE reader a feel for the seriousness of the dialogues that took place around the lunch and breakfast tables. Some rare and insightful moments occurred during these dialogues. Over the years I had taken notes in shorthand and had them transcribed. I have chosen the ones that I think were significant in terms of understanding the teaching or one's *sadhana,* or were important in the light of prevailing political and social issues or in helping one understand the persona of Krishnaji.

Social Justice

ACHYUTJI AND JAGANNATH UPADHYAYA[18] CAME FROM A SOCIALIST background and they would often talk about social justice with Krishnaji. This was especially relevant in the context of the inequalities that prevailed in most societies. They asked whether the teaching provided an answer for the problems faced by the socially marginalized groups.

On one occasion, they asked, "Where does one look for social justice in the teaching?" Krishnaji said, *"Please do not say that the teaching do not consider the 'untouchables,' the underprivileged, and others. First of all, there is no equality* [in this world]. *So instead, ask where is the source, in you, of this duality, of equality and inequality. If we can find that source, then we can deal with our desire to find out where equality, justice, and happiness lie for mankind."*

Achyutji and Jagannath Upadhyaya observed that institutional efforts to bring order and justice have been self-defeating. Both of them had tried all that, and now they had accepted their failure in this direction. Krishnaji pointed out, *"If you admit that institutions cannot alter the world, and that revolutions have not brought about change, and social serv- ice, sympathy, pity, and so forth have not done anything, then, if collective activity has not produced the result, we have to face the truth that all known paths so far have failed, including the collective, to bring equality and justice. If you accept that, only then can we proceed."* He then asked, *"Can I act justly as a human being? Can I act as a human being with equality to another being? Do not say it is impossible. There is compassion that is the only basis for equality and justice. Find out then why you have no compassion."*

Many visitors came from the field of social work, helping the poor and the needy. To one of them he said, *"Receive this teaching with both hands, and then whatever you do will be right action. It won't be a personal action, but whatever comes out of that receiving will be right."*

Negation

DURING THE COURSE OF A DIALOGUE, KRISHNAJI WOULD SOME- times destroy the premise he had built up earlier. He would do that, I felt, in order to break the patterns we tend to create continuously—whether it was a concept, a belief, or a methodology of investigation. This ability of his was clearly demonstrated during a remarkable lunch-table discussion in Vasanta Vihar with Jagannath Upadhyaya. Upadhyaya started questioning K about negation and creation. Upadhyaya said that we use the term *creation* when something comes into being; and in order for something to come into being, there has to be the soil of negation. Negation is a void, and a void cannot create anything. Therefore, there is no causal relationship between void and creativity. For creation to be, there has to be some materiality from which something comes into being. From where does that materiality come into being?

Krishnaji quickly dismissed the basis of this dialogue. He seemed to suggest that negation and creativity were not related. He said, *"Who is going to negate? I do not think there is negation. There is no negation because that implies an entity that negates. It means a subject/object duality exists."* He pointed out, on the other hand, *"If there is a perception in which there is no perceiver, that perception sees. That perception is the whole, and therefore there is no negation."* He further explained that negation meant that there was no holistic perception. If one negated envy, for instance, behind that was the cause to end it. Therefore, there was causation. Krishnaji said, *"I do not negate anything, as there is no such thing as negation. While you,"* he said, *"insist first on negation and then try to negate it."*

He went on to add, *"Whatever is actual cannot be negated because it is 'what is.' 'What is' cannot be negated. I see there is a Frenchman, an Englishman, and so on. That cannot be negated. I know nothing about it. I am not negating it. But I see that in my attempt to divide, there is the fracturing of consciousness."*

The dialogue ended with two insights. One was that if something is a fact, then this fact cannot be negated. The other was that thought divides, but wherever there is a clear perception that "this is so," the duality ends.

At another time, in a personal conversation with me, Krishnaji threw a different light on negation. I asked him about the relationship between nothingness and compassion, about which the Buddha had spoken so much. I said, "I don't know anything about it, but will it be true to say that first comes the state of nothingness and then there is the birth of compassion?" Krishnaji said, *"No, you have got it all wrong. Let us see.*

The brain is the center of all activity, all desire, the whole movement of that. All that content is found within the brain. Anything that happens within that is still held enclosed. As there is negation going on, the very movement of nothingness is compassion. It is not nothingness first and compassion later. The two go together."

There was another conversation on negation between Krishnaji and myself in Calcutta. It was an evening when there was no electricity for a while; candles cast their soft light and shadows, and outside the darkness was gathering. Krishnaji asked me, *"What have you learnt all these years? Are you still a disciple, or are you both the teacher and the disciple?"* I said, "I would say I know what it is to perceive something that arises in consciousness, and the very observation ends that formation. Every such act of perception and negation adds a depth and vitality to the mind. In a small way it is an experience of the ending of time."

Krishnaji said something very revealing: *"Don't you see what you have done? All right, you know what it is to perceive, negate, to end something at the moment of perception, and you say you have been doing this. But don't you see that the whole thing is a process: perception-negation, perception-negation? Process is time, and this way you do not end time. When you say, 'I know the way of negation,' you have brought it within the field of technology, a tool towards something. The moment you learn a process, it is a technological tool, it is time, it is becoming. Stop saying 'I know.' Then the process ends."*

Early Experiences: Theosophical Background

THERE HAS RECENTLY BEEN A LOT OF DISCUSSION ON THE influence of Theosophy on Krishnaji. This dialogue reveals some of his feelings about his early training. This discussion started with the "discipleship" that Krishnaji underwent in the Theosophical Society when he was first discovered on a deserted beach and taken charge of by C. W. Leadbeater,[19] one of the main proponents of Theosophy at that time. On the morning of 25 December 1980, in Vasanta Vihar, Krishnaji was discussing a few questions that some of us had raised:

What does it mean to say that Krishnaji went through the Theosophical phase without being affected? Was he really untouched by

Theosophy, although he used idioms, ideas, and definitions similar to those of the Theosophists? Is it correct to say that what is Theosophical is not just Theosophical, because it is equally Buddhist, Christian, and so on, and so no denominational conditioning went with it? When Krishnaji wrote *At the Feet of the Master*, was he conditioned by his Theosophical training?

Krishnaji began by saying, "*I was not conditioned by the teaching. I mean by this, it came in and it came out. Sir, I would say that they tried to condition me; they tried to say that this is the line you are going to take. They tried to induce me to accept their church, canons, and all that.*" After a moment's reflection he said, "*K had that original thing in Ojai, but he was still within the idiom of Theosophy. I would not call that conditioning. He was learning the languages. I can assure you that none of that mattered. All that thing never touched that boy.*"

A question was asked at this point: "You have never denied that there are Masters." Krishnaji replied, "*What you think of the Master is not what it is. They personalized something immense into personalities.*" One questioner insisted that belief in the Masters was a fundamental part of Theosophy. Krishnaji said, "*Listen to what he [K] is saying. He says C. W. Leadbeater and H. P. Blavatsky[20] made the Masters into something personal. There was certainly a Master here, a Master there, and so on. That was part of Theosophy. But they reduced that immensity to this shoddy little affair.*"

A question was again posed: "It is one thing to say, 'Don't deny immensity,' but it is another thing to say you accept the immensity in Theosophical terms."

Krishnaji said, "*Just a minute. Would you grant that the boy was vague, vacant, totally lost, not there? You came along—C. W. L. or Dr. Besant. You came along and saw the boy had something, you picked the boy up, put him between the two leaders with his brother, and they pour this thing into him, every night—meditation, going to the Masters. The boy repeats all that. Repeats it. It was poured in and poured out.*

"*Now, I would say a totally independent experience took place at Ojai, you follow? That was original, independent, away from the ambience, away from the influence, away from everything that they put into him. I would say that that was the beginning, as that was authentic. Right? But he was still within the idiom of Theosophy, and he broke away ultimately. That's all.*" The conversation ended here. Krishnaji was silent. He did not pursue it.

In another conversation with Achyutji, Krishnaji asked, *"Have you read* Masters on the Path?" Achyutji said, "Yes. I have. I remember everything." Krishnaji said, *"Have you noticed something? Their bodies are refined bodies. But it sounds like an ordinary person when it is said that he has a beard, he has such-and-such color of eyes. It is to corporealize the incorporeal. C. W. L. has distorted the concept of the Masters and brought it to the level of idolatry."*

I am not presuming to represent Krishnaji's relationship to Theosophy or to the Masters. It is too profound and mystical. What do I make of it all? I have no means to know the truth.

Sound and Silence

KRISHNAJI HAS SPOKEN MUCH ON THE SIGNIFICANCE OF SILENCE and sound as when he said, *"Sit under a tree and listen to the sound of a tree trunk."* One day, he said to me, *"I do not know whether you will understand what I am going to say, but write it down:*

> *There is sound with formation*
> *sound without formation,*
> *sound within sound*
> *and sound deep within.*
> *Stay with the sound deep within."*

I asked him whether he could elaborate on all this. Krishnaji replied, *"There are many things which are not talked about."*

One afternoon four or five of us were having lunch with Krishnaji at Vasanta Vihar. Loud music was resounding through the whole neighborhood, as had become a customary practice during the festival times in Madras. Krishnaji began the conversation by asking why we separated sound from silence. One of us pointed out that there was a wide spectrum of responses. At one end of the spectrum existed the one who was in meditative awareness, who had no hopes, no desires, no reactions. At the other extreme end was a person who lived a life propelled by desire, who responded to his wants. In between these two extremes were many indifferent people. Krishnaji said, *"This morning, there was that noise. It was at this end. Does it enter the individual who is in meditative awareness?*

Does that noise enter him with the music? Or does he resist? Or is there no response at all. The fellow at the other end resists. What is the difference between the person who does not resist, and the one who resists, and the other who is totally indifferent?"

A question was then asked, "Is the man who hears and has no resistance also in silence"? Krishnaji said, *"Sound is silence. This morning, Sir, there was music and chanting of the* suprabhatam [a special Sanskrit chant usually associated with the morning hours]. *Both were going on at the top of their voices. I listened to it for a long time. I had no resistance. Therefore, silence is. Therefore, sound is silence. The least resistance would be sound. The fellow who resists all the time is therefore not living in silence. The other fellow, the first fellow, is living in silence. The other person does not even know, he is not bothered about it. Meditation is a form of seeking silence to make the brain silent. Control thought and you have the whole process."*

During another conversation at the lunch table at Vasanta Vihar on January 19, 1985, Krishnaji asked, *"What is sound? Is sound different from silence? There is sound and there is silence. Are they separate, or is silence a part of sound?"* Inquiring into it, he said that there is no silence without sound. *"I want to meditate on silence during silence, you understand? Sir, there is sound when the wind blows among the leaves, there is sound when you people make noise, there is the sound of the birds, there is the sound of my voice. Sound is an extraordinarily important thing. I want people to understand silence. I listen to sound, listen to it, because the universe is sound. Because there is sound, there is silence. They are not two separate things. Sound is in silence. Now, Sir, have you listened to a tree when it is absolutely quiet, listened to the sound of the tree? It is great."*

On Living and Dying

I REMEMBER VERY VIVIDLY A POIGNANT INCIDENT IN DELHI IN 1984. Some of us were at the house of Pupul Jayakar. It was a terrible moment in time. It was the morning when Indira Gandhi was assassinated, October 30, 1984. We heard about it, and there were various reactions from the people gathered there. Some were stunned and bewildered. Some of us stood silently, grave and sorrowful. It was an immensely tragic event, and for some time there was a shocked silence.

A little later conversation started; many questions were posed about who would become the next prime minister, who were the king-makers, and other issues concerning the political future of the country. Yet death was there, palpable and pervading. I saw how difficult it was for us to hold on to that moment of suffering, and because it was painful, too painful, the mind sought relief in some activity, in frivolity, or irrelevant thoughts. To live with that extraordinary poignancy of suffering for a long duration was difficult.

Krishnaji was there, watching us all. He was looking out into the garden where the dewdrops on the grass were reflecting the sunlight. He said to us, "*Look there! That is life. There is death here, and there is life there. That is the whole movement; life and death go together.*" He added, "*It is a day of mourning for the living, not for the dead. She is gone. Life goes on. Look at the sunlight and trees and the bushes...life goes on.*"

It was an extraordinary thing to say what he did at that time when the atmosphere was so emotionally charged. He brought sanity and perspective into the occasion. He helped us to see death not as an isolated single act but as part of the movement of life.

On Good and Evil

KRISHNAJI SPOKE OF A RESERVOIR OF GOODNESS WAITING TO touch human beings. This goodness had nothing to do with the pairs of opposites as good and bad. Good and bad are relative, they are social values, whereas goodness per se has no relationship to the opposite — it is beyond value. Of evil, Krishnaji said, "*Evil exists, but you don't know anything about it.*"

By evil Krishnaji seemed to imply the thoughts and actions that arise out of violence, envy, and the will to hurt. He felt that it was essential to keep one's consciousness free of such thoughts and feelings. One day when I was telling him stories about a charlatan kind of a guru, he told me, "*Don't even think or talk about such evil people. By thinking and talking about them, you make it [evil] stronger. Don't allow entry to it.*"

I can now understand why the *mandalas* for protection came into existence. They prevent the seeds of evil taking root in the soil of our consciousness; they are the lines of protection. Of *mandalas*, Krishnaji told a few of us, "It has so often happened to me that I have been to homes where I have felt unpleasantness or evil. I then walk around the room to create a protective circle. You call it 'mandala'; the Theosophists use the term 'tiling the room.' The 'tiling' shuts out all evil influences. Then my body is at peace and can rest."

A question was raised, "What is the seed of degeneration that exists in human consciousness that grows and wipes away all the good?" Krishnaji probed into the question of this destructive seed that seemed to have more power than good. He stated, "One spot of evil seems to be far more powerful than the good. So what is this factor in human beings, which, although exposed to the good [to the teaching], corrodes and destroys that good?"

He then went on to say a strange thing: "Do you know, that in Co-Masonry it is believed that after the thirty-third initiation, two angels appear in order to protect you anytime you need them? When evil touches you, these angels come and look after you. But you are supposed to live a way of life which does not demand their presence." He further added, "Do you know that C. W. L. used to say that arrogance, power, self-importance, selfishness, and hate are black powers? To have any one of these is to have the seed."

It seems to me from his words that one has to try, scrupulously and attentively, to clip the arising of self-importance, the taste for power and position, and the stealthy movement of vanity. These tendencies corrupt the mind. To eliminate the seed of corruption is part of a religious way of life.

I said, "Krishnaji, you are asking us to act from there, the 'other,' to touch that, and then everything that we do will be right. What is the relationship of this field of good and evil to the 'other'? Is evil transformed through negation?" Krishnaji replied, "No, you have to negate the whole of this field with all its good and evil. In this is evil, power, arrogance, selfishness. Then the other is good, man trying to better the world, social work—the whole of that. The good is always the feebler, the weaker, as compared with the other. Evil overcomes the good. Good action has to go on. Let us call that good action done with a cause, with a motive, with a direction. But you have to understand that the whole of that, both the evil and the good with a cause, are within one area, the known. The 'other' is beyond this duality."

KRISHNAJI AND
THE ORGANIZATION

WHY DID KRISHNAJI ESTABLISH THE VARIOUS FOUNDATIONS? What was his relationship to them? Krishnaji's relationship to organizations has been rather ambivalent. He left the Theosophical Society, for he felt no religious organization could lead to the truth. Yet, paradoxically, he established centers in different parts of the world. What impelled him to do this?

As I see it, first Krishnaji was associated with two organizations— one, the Theosophical Society in his early life, and the other, the K foundations, the schools, and the study centers. The Theosophical Society had its specific goals, structure, ceremonies, and rituals. For nearly two decades, he was an integral part of it, and one can even say he was the focal point of its activities. My observation from what I have read and heard is that he was not directly connected with the manner and method of its management. His life seemed to move in a different sphere, a closed and protected orbit, in the midst of an international Theosophical network.

A fundamental change took place when he came to India after the war years. I do not have any personal acquaintance with those intervening years, 1929 to 1947. From the extant records, it is clear that after he left the Theosophical Society in 1929, another group of people looked after him from 1930 onwards. They took charge of his personal needs, the arrangement of tours and talks, and the management of his financial affairs. He seemed, again, to have had very little, if any, part in the way these affairs were managed. He trusted these people unquestioningly and seemed to have accepted the manner in which they managed the organization.

In 1947, Krishnaji, contrary to his past dealings with the Foundation, took complete charge of organizational matters in India, including the direction the schools should take. The then-members of the Rishi Valley Trust resigned en bloc, enabling him to reconstitute the trust as he wished, including inducting new members. The Rishi Valley Trust later became the Foundation for New Education and finally evolved into the KFI. It was a movement from non-involvement to involvement. Between 1968 and 1969, he broke his connection with the KWINC. I think it was this parting of the ways with Rajagopal that gave an impetus to his establishing the various Krishnamurti foundations. It was at that time that the Krishnamurti Foundation Trust, Krishnamurti Foundation of America, and Krishnamurti Foundation India also came into being. He did not regard the foundations as religious organizations; they were established essentially for the dissemination of the teaching.

KRISHNAJI'S RELATIONSHIP WITH THE FOUNDATIONS

KRISHNAJI DID NOT LOOK UPON THE FOUNDATION AS A religious organization with a hierarchical structure. He regarded it as a functional body established to spread the teaching by making available to the public books, videos, and audiotapes. Neither the Foundation nor any member was to be a successor to the teacher or the teaching. No one was to inherit the mantle. At the end of his life, he had expressed the wish that the purity of the teaching was to be kept intact and that there should be no distortion. He consistently maintained throughout his life that there should be no interpreters of the teaching. There could be dialogues and discussions, but no one had the authority to speak in his name. There was neither temple nor dogma to be built around him and the teaching. He held that it was the primary function of the Foundation to preserve the purity of the teaching.

Why did K categorically maintain that no organization could be religious? It can be observed that no organization can be said to have been religious. Only people in an organization can be religious. Throughout history, religious organizations have been sectarian, divisive, and hierarchical. Krishnaji was firm in categorically stating that the Foundation was not a religious body.

Then the question arises, what is the responsibility of the members? Is it merely to publish books, spread the teaching, and manage the schools? K held that each member's primary responsibility was to live the teaching. I felt he expected members to be worthy of the trust that was inherent in their being in the Foundation. It was almost a sacred duty to discover what it meant to lead a holistic life, moving in that direction, never losing touch with the spirit of self-inquiry. He spoke of members being able to absorb the teaching and be authentic to his or her insights. As I look at it, by historical accident or personal destiny, over the years people came into the Foundation or into his orbit and did whatever was needed at that time. I felt that the commitment he expected from all of us was to live the teaching in daily life.

Krishnaji felt that Foundation members were linked together by their being invested with this sacred responsibility. If any misunderstandings arose, he felt that they should be discussed and resolved immediately, as otherwise it would vitiate the spirit of the Foundation. For instance, when there were strained working relations between some colleagues, he wrote to me, urging, "*You should all work together, help each other to grow, to flower. If there are any misunderstandings among you, as there are sure to be, they should be dissolved immediately by talking things over, and not postponed to the next day or even the next hour. If postponed, the misunderstandings will grow and become barriers between you. I would most strongly urge you, if I may, not to keep each other's work in separate, watertight compartments. We are all working together, either externally or inwardly.*"

Again, on another occasion when there was some estrangement between two colleagues, he said that such relationships should never be broken. As they were part of the Foundation, he felt they were beyond the personal, something much greater and as such, he felt the bond could not be broken. "*You have come together sharing in common something profound, as seekers after truth. You should keep your hearts open.*" This was the kind of harmony he wanted to weave between the Foundation members. He felt that as members, as individuals who were together in search of truth, they were bound together. Such a bond was a sacred one that could enkindle the flame of insight, not in isolation but in being, communicating, and working together.

WORKING IN THE ORGANIZATION

INHERENT IN ANY ORGANIZATION IS POWER. NEARNESS TO Krishnaji can be heady. It gave one self-importance and one easily and unconsciously became a victim of the movements of self-projection and power. These movements were so subtle that one had to be constantly vigilant. The urge to identify oneself with the place or position, one's self projection, had to be observed and negated; he felt this was essential in order to preserve the sanctity of the place. Living in the midst of power conflicts and schisms, this was a constant challenge.

Krishnaji invested care and detail in every project he undertook. He seemed to seek a perfect harmony and expected it of others who worked for him. Slipshod work would not be tolerated, nor would he accept my defenses or excuses for something not done. One had to be punctual to the minute. As he used to say, if there was no order outwardly, there would be no inner order either, because they go together. He was not a person to praise you or pat you on the back. It was understood that this was part of one's role of being in the place.

This demand of the totality of one's energies created many dilemmas for Krishnaji and the members. For instance, a person could become slack, losing the original vitality and drive. Then the place suffered. He dealt with people and such situations in different ways. At such times, two different streams seemed to have operated within him. One was surgical and harsh, and the other was compassionate. He would say that whatever decision was taken must be right for the person as well as the place, and if the person had to go, then so be it. Many people thus left their positions of responsibility in his lifetime.

In such a situation, one went through feelings of rejection, disappointment, and failure. In the final event, it was not a question of being approved or disapproved, found adequate or not, nor was it relevant to ruminate whether things were fair or not. For what was right for the place had to prevail.

WERE KRISHNAJI'S DECISIONS IN THE FOUNDATION INFLUENCED?

WAS KRISHNAJI INFLUENCED IN HIS DECISIONS? HOW MUCH credence did he give to other people's views, judgments, and assessments? Generally, people around him had a feeling that he was influenced and that some persons were able to use their nearness to him in ways that colored his judgments of people and matters in the Foundation.

In 1980, when we were in Saanen for the gathering, after a lunch with him at Chalet Tannegg, I was with him in his room having an easy conversation about both little things and serious matters. In the course of the conversation, I asked him "Krishnaji, why do you get influenced by some people? It is X in India and Y abroad." He did not seem to mind my asking such a question, nor did he think it intrusive. He thought it over for a while, then said, *"No, I don't think I am being influenced. When K was a boy, so much was poured into him, and it came out. He obeyed the instructions given to him. He was a weak boy, physically. He trusted people."* He continued to say that as he grew up, from the twenties onwards, he started questioning everything around him. However, it was really when the Rajagopal episode took place and he felt betrayed by someone whom he had trusted implicitly that he woke up. *"From that time onwards, I have been very watchful. I listen to what others say, but finally I do what I see is right. No, I am not being influenced."*

Pondering over this, and being a witness for decades to the many happenings in the Indian and other foundations, I tentatively observe that he may have been influenced temporarily in certain matters. But deep down, it seemed he could never be touched or influenced. Sometimes, though some members did not accept his views and suggestions initially, in the final analysis his wish would prevail. He gave one a long rope, and when things did not progress as expected, then he would intervene and somehow see to it that action was taken, as he thought fit.

When I look back at the time when he had decided that Pamaji and I should leave Vasanta Vihar, he was very affectionate and tender, but he told me that I had to be fully aware of my actions and that time had run out. Perhaps he felt that we were not in a position to give Vasanta Vihar the religious spirit that he thought it required. Perhaps the place needed a change of persons. When he said all this to Pamaji and me, was he influenced? Yes and no. It was his perception. I saw that. Krishnaji did have that quality of seeing our inadequacies in terms of the teaching. What he asked from one was a total transformation in oneself. So neither Pamaji nor I felt devastated because of what he said. Yet it did not mean that there were no influences being brought upon him. Those influences probably strengthened his view and directed the manner in which action followed. These factors made the experience unpleasant. In some cases he could act decisively, but in others he seemed to be helpless in spite of his strong feelings that things were not being done correctly.

Krishnaji was such a towering personality with an overwhelming spiritual presence that one granted to him the right to correct, reject, or modify as he thought best. It may have been difficult at that moment for one to accept it, but later, on reflection, one felt that one's ego was in operation, subtly, and that he, the teacher, had the right to point it out. It seemed to work towards one's inner growth. After all, one entered the Foundation not to seek power and self-importance but to deepen one's understanding of the self. So though his actions appeared severe, it seemed to help us mature within.

MY PREDICAMENT

MANY QUESTIONS ARISE AS I LOOK AT THAT TEN-YEAR CYCLE OF events from this distance of time. What did the movement of years unfold to me, about the place, myself, the personalities in the Foundation, and the organizational pressures that were inherent in such a situation? What was happening to me during all these years of activities and responsibility? Was there something more that was expected of me? Something deeper and more profound than all that I did? Was I fully conscious of my responsibilities and duties, my capacities and inadequacies? It was like a karmic circle of which I was a part. The waters I sailed in were stormy and clouded. I was often torn between powerful schisms within the Foundation. I lost my moorings, and consequently my actions were confused.

My position as a functionary in the organizational context brought with it tremendous responsibilities. Pamaji had to manage the place, and I had a special assignment of giving the place a religious feeling. What did this mean to me when I began my work in Vasanta Vihar? I often wondered what more could I do when Krishnaji himself was the "spirit" of the place. Yet he had given me a special responsibility; in fact, he had chosen me for that. I looked at my situation and found that my role was varied. One was my role as a *sadhaka* (one who practices spiritual disciplines); then there was the organizational responsibility, to look after the place, reflect friendliness despite antagonisms; to be worldly and at the same time be grounded on the "other." Could all these demands be met? There was always the image of the enlightened consciousness of Krishnaji in front of me, which I identified as a model. Perhaps this image influenced me unconsciously and came in the way of looking at myself? I did not seem to have the maturity to penetrate the various conflicts nor the strength to stand firmly on my beliefs and live by my perceptions. A few of these confusions seemed to rise from the contradictions embedded in the context of my location. The teacher as the head of the organization demanded right action at the pragmatic and organizational levels, and at the same time called for an integral response from within that was not ego-based. Then there were the various self-motivated movements from individual members who were part of the organizational ethos. Finally, there was the solid ground of affection between K and myself, which was the most precious blessing and yet this impelled me to demand more of myself than I had to give. It also gave one a false awareness of one's position that led to a growing sense of self-importance and self-projecting tendencies, which was disquieting. These opposing configurations and forces led to inward turmoil. Naturally, I felt I could not measure up to the task that lay ahead of me.

I said to Krishnaji once, "I am doing my best, but it is not enough. I feel I am inadequate." He said laughingly, *"Your best is peanuts,"* and then added, *"There is no such thing as being adequate. You can never be adequate; it is all too big, but be profoundly aware."* To be aware meant so many things. I was not to act out of a feeling of inadequacy. It was the "me" which has to be absent in relationships and actions.

What he wanted of me or any of us who had listened to him and taken the teaching seriously was to be a light unto oneself. It may not be a flame, but it could be candlelight. Light is light. He said, *"If you are all right, then people will come to you like bees to honey."* A compassionate person touches the hearts of people. Did I have it? Do I have it? Do we all, who speak of being religious, have that goodness of compassion?

INTERRUPTIONS
AND CHANGES

FOR NEARLY SEVEN YEARS, EVENTS WERE MOVING WELL. Krishnaji's yearly visits, publications, and all other activities went off well and there were no manifest, serious tensions. But gradually dissatisfaction came to be expressed by him, and a feeling that there was a need for a change at Vasanta Vihar. The first attempt to change things was in 1983 but nothing came out of it. We offered to resign at that time, but we had to continue at Vasanta Vihar, as there was no one else to take over.

Krishnaji expected one to do all the things required for the place and remain inward. He would ask me, for instance, *"What is happening to you? You have not come here just to look after all this. What is happening to your mind? Are you deeply aware?"*

Unless one was ever-diligent, watching oneself like a hawk at what was happening inwardly, one would find it almost impossible to face the immense responsibility. In any organization there were bound to be conflicts, power plays, schisms, tense relationships, and so on. Krishnaji was deeply concerned about members working together and trusting in each other. He considered, for instance, that my relationship with Pupulji was important for the functioning of the Foundation. So even when differences arose between us, he urged me to mend the relationship.

Brockwood Park
June 24, 1977

My dear Sunanda,
...Now with regard to your confidential letter of the 15th, look, Sunanda, I meant what I said. I said to you and Pama that you should treat Vasanta Vihar as the Headquarters of the Foundation and also treat it as your home—and I mean it. But I also said, "Don't take root in the place." I mean by that, please do not become attached to it....If one

becomes "attached," then the place will lose its perfume. That is what happened with the previous management... This is just a warning, and I hope you will understand, and in any case I still say to you and Pama, "Treat it as your home," but if I may point out most gently, do not get identified with the buildings or property.

Then the other point is that you and Pupul must get on absolutely in harmony. I know there are some misunderstandings between you and her. I saw it when I was last in Bombay. If I may suggest, slur over all the past hurts and misunderstandings and disagreements, and please, Sunanda, see the importance that you and Pupul must get on really well together. In the moment of anger or irritation we say things we do not quite mean, so let those moments pass by and do not recall them. I am giving you grandfatherly advice and hope you understand what I mean.

J.K.

It was indeed timely advice for one to learn to live without pettiness, to slur over the hurts and not to recall. It did help me in my interaction with Pupulji and with my other colleagues, relatives, and friends. This emptying process becomes the source of freshness in daily living.

During these years I also had to face difficult challenges in my marital life, some of which emanated from my responsibilities and functions in the Foundation. Krishnaji often used to talk to me about Foundation matters although it was Pamaji who was secretary of the Foundation. He used to tell Pamaji, *"I have talked it over with Sunanda; she will discuss it with you."* It was not easy for anyone to accept a situation where one's role was superseded. It was my nearness to Krishnaji that gave rise to these unpleasant comparisons. Our marriage would have developed cracks but for a strong relationship based on mutual respect and affection. I feel that in every marriage there are occasions where there can be jealousy and comparisons between a couple. What sustains such relationships is trust in each other, an understanding of each other, and an abiding affection that can take on all these storms of life. There were also other factors that helped us over these patches; our shared awareness of these incidents lessened them, and furthermore we felt our pettiness being washed away in Krishnaji's presence. For when we are open to the vibrations of an enlightened person, we do go through a kind of purification. His presence and our perceptions had helped us continuously over the years.

THE FINAL MONTHS: MADRAS, 1985/1986

THE LAST FAREWELL

I WOULD LIKE TO NARRATE IN DETAIL SOME OF THE EVENTS OF K's last visit to India. It was significant in many ways, as numerous decisions were taken that affected my life and that of the Foundation. The narrative assumes the form of a journal, marking time, as it were, until the end.

In November 1985, when Krishnaji came to Delhi on his yearly visit, I started keeping a day-to-day taped account of the conversations and happenings that were taking place in the Indian Foundation and elsewhere. When I look back upon this peculiar and inexplicable phenomenon of my talking into the tape, which I had not done with such consistency ever before, I am amazed at my own actions of that time. Krishnaji spent nearly two months between New Delhi, Rajghat, Madras, and Rishi Valley before he abruptly ended his stay in India and proceeded to Ojai in January 1986.

Why did I feel like keeping meticulously recorded notes of the day-to-day unfolding situations and Krishnaji's conversations with me? I now see that there must have been some premonition that that year was going to be extremely significant to me personally and to the Foundation. How true it all turned out to be.

For ten years, 1986/1996, I put away the tapes in a cupboard. Never have I even once played them, heard them, or even thought about them. I had forgotten about them. Now that I have entered my seventies, I feel an urgency to tie up all loose ends, to put down whatever record I have about myself in relation to the teacher, to the teaching, and the Foundation. I feel that an authentic and personal report of the last visit of Krishnaji would be significant at this time.

Two unpredictable events marked this trip. The first was that this was to be Krishnaji's last visit to India, as it was followed very soon by his passing away on February 17, 1986 at Ojai, just a month after he left India. The other event was that this was another turning point in my personal life. Pamaji and I were to leave Vasanta Vihar, and this decision had to be taken with Krishnaji's consent.

The entries contain accounts of Krishnaji's deteriorating health, the changeable states of his mind, and his thoughts on some matters related to the Foundation. He seemed to be suffering tremendous pain while he was in India, and I could see this clearly at Vasanta Vihar.

Listening to the tapes, I feel that he was acutely aware of his mortality. This perhaps made him restless and brought with it an urgency to settle matters in the Foundation. Many decisions were taken at that time, and Krishnaji seemed under great pressure. Numerous problems were sorted out regarding the Foundation, and towards the end of the visit he felt that he should be disassociated from all organizational matters.

EXTRACTS FROM
RECORDED NOTES

New Delhi, October 27, 1985

KRISHNAJI ARRIVED IN DELHI ON 25TH MORNING. WHEN I met him two days later, he looked extremely frail. His mind seemed to be far away from India. I felt he was somehow different that year.

Some of us were discussing with him about the world situation. At the end of an hour's conversation in the morning, he was able to see that there were great complexities to the political and economic situation in India. At the end of the conversation, Krishnaji raised the question: What is the future of mankind? Then that quality which was so much Krishnaji entered. He started talking about conditioning and the future of human-ity. *"Is there any solution to the human condition? Will there be peace? How does it come about? We are trying to solve problems through organi-zation, social reform, welfare work, but these will never solve the problems of man. The crisis is in the individual, in the human being and not in organization."*

Rajghat, November 4, 1985

I FOUND KRISHNAJI RATHER AGITATED. HE SEEMS TO HAVE MADE up his mind about some matters relating to Vasanta Vihar. He felt that I had not discharged the responsibilities he had entrusted to me. Vasanta Vihar, he stated, had not become a religious place. It was not possible to respond, for he seemed to have come to certain definite conclusions. At one level, he would point out that I had not done this and that, but then there would come a flash of compassion, an intimacy of communication, of great beauty. He would say something extraordinarily profound in the midst of the conversation, communicating a different dimension that helped me see the whole picture, and every reaction in oneself got wiped out. If I had reacted to him even in a small measure, my ego would have entered it with defensive argument and that would be the end of communication. Therefore, I allowed everything to flow in.

Rajghat, November 6, 1985

HE WAS TALKING TO ME ABOUT MYSELF. AFTER TELLING ME something about what was happening to me, he ended the conversation. Then, as he sat on the bench in the verandah, putting on his shoes, ready to go out for a walk, he said, *"Sunanda, I have talked to you about so many things. Listen. Sunanda is dead. It is no longer a matter of 'I am doing this,' but we are all together doing it."* That was his message, his benediction, whatever words we may use for that grace. I felt this deeply from the depths of my heart.

Vasanta Vihar, November 9, 1985

A MUSIC CONCERT WAS HELD IN VASANTA VIHAR. PUPUL CAME and sat next to me and said, *"I am rather worried, Sunanda. Krishnaji has said he is not going to live long. He seems very wobbly on his feet this evening. If anything happens to him here…"* So, before the end of the concert, Pupul, Nandini, and I left the music hall and went to Krishnaji's room. He was sitting on his bed having his dinner. Pupulji asked him with concern, "How are you?" He said, *"I am not dead yet. I am just a bit too tired. That's all."* So, the three of us stood quiet for a few minutes and came away.

I felt deeply disturbed last night, heavy with the feeling that Krishnaji was not going to live long. Reflecting on the nature of my work and relationships during the last ten years, particularly with regard to making Vasanta Vihar religious, I see I am caught in a strange situation. While on the one hand he continues to say that I have not done this, done that, and one is not living the teaching, he also says, *"Don't leave."* What am I to do? So I told myself, "Just listen to him. The many events and pressures that are happening around him are part of *lila* [the divine play]—passing and ephemeral. I should not be drowned in it."

Vasanta Vihar, November 15, 1985

I WENT TO HIS ROOM TO SAY GOODBYE, AS HE WAS LEAVING FOR Rishi Valley. He said, "*Come, sit down. I want to tell you something. Did you notice what happened this morning? Did you see what is happening right in front of my nose? The discussion is all about function and money. Where is the teaching? It has always been like this historically; see it. I am talking of something, and the Foundation is talking of function; you are separating the two. The division between function and the spirit of the thing is not the teaching.*"

Rishi Valley, November 22, 1985

AT RISHI VALLEY ONE DAY, I SAID TO KRISHNAJI, "IT IS VERY strange that I discovered certain things about myself. First, I have to die to all my traumatic experiences. Krishnaji, let me go back in time. In 1947, I met you, and for seven or eight years, I was doing fourteen hours of work a day as your official stenographer. During all those years, I had no difficulty of communication with you. But in the last two or three years, things have changed."

Krishnaji said, "*I am telling you, wipe out the past. Wipe out everything and start over.*" He said, "*You have talked to me. So let us start afresh all over. You have to wipe it out.*" I then got up. He said, "*Look, this is the last time I am saying it; you have to take full responsibility for Vasanta Vihar. I am saying all this, I won't say it again.*"

And I said, "Sir, I realize that I have to be totally alone, not seeking alliances, security in certain relationships in this context."

"*At last,*" he said, "*you are seeing this.*"

I came back with the feeling that he was still entrusting Vasanta Vihar into my hands and that I had to act. I was thinking about the impossible requirements that he had posed to me, like "*You have not done it, you have not made Vasanta Vihar a religious place, and you will have to do it. You have to be tremendously responsible from now on and wipe out all the past.*" I don't know what it means to create a religious place. Can I really say I don't know and find out the shallowness of that statement?

Vasanta Vihar, December 25, 1985

I WENT TO KRISHNAJI'S ROOM TO CHECK WHETHER THINGS were in order and comfortable. He was lying down. He said, *"Sit down, Sunanda, listen, I have lost five to six pounds. I will immediately have to leave India. Do you realize the seriousness of it?"* I was looking deeply into his eyes. He held my hands, and there was a great deal of unspoken communication while he was saying this. I was suddenly deeply grieved and afraid of the import of what he was saying. *"Look, the body is not picking up, and I may have to be taken on a stretcher. I won't have it. Bombay is out; I will leave for Ojai. I cannot stand the cold of England. It is warm here. Rishi Valley was cold. The body needs warmth without a sweater; then it feels well."* He said, *"Look, the body is going. It may not last long. I will have to settle everything. I have settled Rishi Valley, Rajghat, and there is something unfinished at Ojai. I must go back before I fall ill and get grounded here."*

I was listening to him with a deep weight in the pit of my stomach because I knew that the time was nearing. I said, "Sir, I feel it is necessary to see a doctor here this afternoon. After all, nothing is lost. If something is wrong, we can treat it. If you have the energy, would you consider?" He said, *"All right."* He kept quiet. Half an hour later when I went to see him again, he said, *"Yes, I have talked to Dr. Parchure, and he said yes. So fix it."*

Vasanta Vihar, December 27, 1985

DR. THIRUVENGADAM, A PHYSICIAN OF RARE EMINENCE WHOM I had requested to attend K, rang me up and spoke to me, saying that Krishnaji's prostate should be examined. Nobody except for half a dozen people in the world knew that Krishnaji had cancer earlier. Therefore, when he was losing weight rapidly it was a situation of alarm and concern. Krishnaji insisted, *"I will not be examined by any doctor here. Even when Dr. Thiruvengadam examined me, my body was quivering. I don't want to be touched. I want to be examined by my own doctor in Los Angeles."*

Vasanta Vihar, December 29 and 30, 1985

AT FOUR O'CLOCK IN THE EVENING, I WENT UP TO HIS ROOM TO see him. He was sitting on his cot and started talking. He felt that he would cancel some of his programs and then leave for Ojai, a little earlier than planned, on January 12. Then Scott came into the room and said, "Many people come to see you here, and I will stand at the door and prevent people from coming in. I will guard the door." I said, "Please, you don't do anything of that kind here. We are looking after him." Krishnaji turned round and said to Scott, *"In India I will never close my doors. I can't say no to people. I have always been like that. It is all right."*

Later Dr. Parchure and I agreed with him. Krishnaji should do whatever he wanted. There was no point in having enforced rest for him. That evening he came down for a walk, very late, and there were one hundred people waiting to have his *darshan* (blessing of a sage). He greeted them all, went for a walk, and returned soon. Even in frail health he was sensitive to the needs of other individuals around him and felt he should discharge his responsibilities as far as he could.

Vasanta Vihar, January 5, 1986

KRISHNAJI ASKED ME, *"SUNANDA, TELL ME VERY SIMPLY, NOT IN your roundabout Tamilian way of talking* [Krishnaji often made fun of me]. *Tell me simply."* He said, *"The Indian mind says all kinds of things except gives a direct answer. It is like an Italian: if you asked an Italian how to reach the other village, he would say, 'Go straight, and then turn left, and then a little there, ten yards of that, go towards the right, and then left.' Then he would ask how much time you have?" Everything except the direct answer."* I liked the way he talked. We both laughed.

Krishnaji was reclining on the back of the cot. He looked extraordinarily beautiful. One was not even aware that he had fever at that time. He did not seem to be aware that he was ill. He began to talk, *"He* [referring to himself] *said that the computer and genetic engineering are going to change human behavior. Then what are you going to do? What is it that he conveyed to you in the talk? He also talked about life, the origin of life, and that there is no beginning, you can never know the beginning."* I started to say something. He said, *"Keep quiet."* Again, he went on to ask what I got out of the talk. And before I could answer, he started speaking again. With Krishnaji, one must never interrupt him.

Then he asked me to say what I wanted to communicate earlier. So I said, "Krishnaji, two years ago I did not realize that the time has come for us to leave Vasanta Vihar and allow others to carry out what you wanted to happen there. Last year I could have told you this, but I thought that if I said that to you, then you may think that I am going away in reaction to what you had said then. Even now, when you told me in Rishi Valley that you are leaving Vasanta Vihar to me, I hesitated. But I know now, whatever you may say, the right thing for me to do is to leave this place."

He said, "*Sunanda, are you quite sure that you are saying this not out of any pressure, not out of any motivation, not due to force of circumstances? Are you doing this without any reason?*"

I said, "Krishnaji, it is not that I have not talked to people. It is not that I do not know what others feel, but that has nothing to do with my decision. My decision is final, and it is right for me to leave." Then he asked again, "*Are you sure you are not doing it out of pressure or motivation? Does it mean that you are leaving the Foundation?*"

I said that this act of mine was complete in itself. "As far as leaving the Foundation is concerned, I am not leaving the Foundation unless you want me to do so." He said, "*No, no, don't leave. I just wanted to know. That means, where will you stay.*" I said, "I will stay in Madras and rent an apartment or a house." Then he said, "*Find a house near the beach.*" He was compassionate and asked me, "*What do you want to do now?*" I said I did not know, but perhaps I might talk, dialogue, and share with others whatever understanding of life I have. He said, "*Do it.*" Then he said something very beautiful: "*At the age of ninety or ninety-one, if someone were to ask me what I would like to do, I will go back; have a lovely car, probably a beautiful Mercedes. Then I will go for a drive with the wind blowing, I will watch the mountains, the sky, the stars. What's wrong? I would love to do it.*"

I thought he had finished talking and so kept quiet. But after a while he started talking again. He said, "*This was to be the last talk which he will ever give, and he is gone. What have you got out of it?*" I told him what I felt about the talk. I added that I did not understand what he said about creation, but there was something indescribably sacred in the atmosphere.

I went to Krishnaji's room before his evening walk and helped him to put on his *kurta*. I told him that I would like to have five minutes after his return from the walk. Later I went up to his room to meet him. He sat on his bed and I also sat on the bed facing him.

"*Now, tell me,*" he said. I started by saying, "Krishnaji, I want to tell you something. I think it is the right thing for me to leave Vasanta Vihar. I would like to leave because this place has to be free for whosoever comes here to do what they want to do. I have done my bit."

Krishnaji said, "*So, you are leaving this place. Will you be connected with Madras school and all that?*"

I said, "Krishnaji, I have not thought about all that. The first thing for me is to leave and see what happens."

Then Krishnaji asked whether I was very clear that I was not leaving with any bitterness or resentment, without ill will to the place. I said, "Krishnaji, for thirty-eight years I have seen this happening—a person leaving a place, a K place, and getting bitter and angry or nursing resentment. I hope I do not have any such feelings. I go with all goodwill, but it will take time to digest this."

He said, "*I am so glad that you feel that you are leaving with a great deal of goodwill. That's good.*" Then he said, "*You should gather yourself in greater attention; it's like a perfume. Recent events have disturbed you. Your mind is not stable. Unless it is stable, it will be lost in this search for something beyond the brain. Only That matters.*" That was his blessing, I felt. He embraced me and said, "*Be well.*"

Vasanta Vihar, January 9, 1986

THE EVENING BEFORE HE WAS TO LEAVE FOR OJAI, HE CALLED Pamaji and me to meet him in his room. Three members of the Foundation were also present. He told us, almost commanded us, to stay on in Vasanta Vihar even though we may not be holding any position. I said to him that it was no longer right to stay on. Despite what two of the other members said, I repeated that our decision was final. It was accepted.

Vasanta Vihar, January 10, 1986

WHEN HE LEFT VASANTA VIHAR SOON AFTER MIDNIGHT FOR THE airport on the tenth, he was looking very ill. He seemed to be far away from everything around him. Some said that they did not feel any contact with him at the time of his leaving. He certainly was very critically ill and yet never showed it. Until the end he continued with his schedule and carried out everything he had to do. The body was used as a vehicle for the teaching until the very end. What an extraordinary teacher and a person he was.

Vasanta Vihar, February 1986

KRISHNAJI PASSED AWAY AT OJAI ON FEBRUARY 17, 1986. PAMAJI AND I went to Delhi to bring Krishnaji's ashes to Vasanta Vihar. The urn containing his ashes was kept on a specially constructed platform (a temporary structure) under the canopy of the trees where he used to give the public talks. For three days, people came from all over the city to pay their homage.

On a beautiful sunny morning, Narayan, Krishna, and Pamaji carried the urn with Krishnaji's ashes and immersed it in the ocean along the shores of the Theosophical Society. It was on this very beach that Krishnaji was discovered in 1909, to fulfill his destiny as one of the greatest religious teachers of our times. Seventy-seven years later in the same place, his ashes mingled with the waters of the ocean.

INTERLUDE

SOME FACETS
OF KRISHNAJI

OFTEN SINCE K'S PASSING AWAY, PEOPLE HAVE ASKED ME, "What kind of person was K? What were his habits, his likes, his dislikes? Was he psychic?" I would therefore like to narrate some anecdotes that show different facets of his personality.

Krishnaji was very much human. We often do not expect him to be so, for we imagine a person of enlightenment to be all sorts of things. We are quite surprised and shocked when the image we had did not merge with what one saw. He had many facets, some paradoxical and some even contradictory. He was compassionate and yet seemed remote and harsh in his relationships. He appeared aloof, yet when one knew him he could be close and easily approachable. Distant and near, affectionate and admonishing, he was a person of whom one could never really say, "I have known him." There was something in him that, one felt, could never be touched or understood. That "otherness" gave his actions and behavior at different times and different levels an unknowable quality. That's why I could never make any judgment or remarks about him, although I was aware of the apparent contradictions.

And what was the nature of my relationship with Krishnaji? I did certainly have a good relationship with him. There was affection and a complete vulnerability to him on my part. Yet there was always a sense that I never really knew him. He could say to me, "*Sunanda, we are friends. If I am senile and you observe it, you must tell me.*" There was that kind of openness, and yet he was, in a deep sense, unknowable.

I once asked him, "Krishnaji, what is my relationship with you?" What he said in reply throws some light on what one could or could not expect from him: "*Sunanda, I am like the wind. Can you hold the wind in your fist? I am like that. There is nothing to hold. That's why I am telling you, don't be attached to me. I have told others too, not to be attached to me.*"

I told him that I saw clearly that there was no personal relationship with him. This was not like any other normal relationship of affection. I said, "For instance, if someone close to me died, I could not come to you for solace." He said, "*You are putting it wrongly. Don't put it that way. I have affection for people. But I say, don't get attached to me, as I am like the wind; you can't hold it. There is nothing to hold.*"

Yet there was something else that he said to me later that gave me a sense of strength and support. It was something of a "mystical" nature: *"Do the right thing, and I will be always there with you."*

Another observation I have made is that during the many years that I had known him, I felt that he seemed to have no attachment to anyone. I am not talking of his earlier years, but the years after I met him. He could pour affection on an individual and have compassion for one. But he did not seem to communicate attachment.

Krishnaji had the quality of giving total attention to whatever he undertook. For instance, when he was at a particular place, say Rishi Valley or Vasanta Vihar, he was totally there, looking into every little detail, attending to problems, meeting people with affection. But a day or so before he left that place, there seemed to be some kind of withdrawal, an emptying, as it were, of relationships to that place and the people around it. Probably that is why he seemed to have no attachment as we know it. He appeared to be alone, somewhere else, far away.

PSYCHIC POWERS

KRISHNAJI'S BIOGRAPHERS HAVE OFTEN WRITTEN ABOUT THE many psychic powers he had, such as healing, telepathy, reading other people's thoughts or reading the contents of a letter without opening the envelope. I have known him to heal some people, including myself. In 1969, I was ill with a very severe attack of rheumatoid arthritis. But for his healing "passes," I would have been crippled years ago. In later years, Krishnaji stopped healing people physically. He said it is much more important to heal psychologically. By this he meant living a right kind of life. He would say that it is easy to acquire *siddhis* (paranormal powers). He felt that these powers were a deviation for a person who is interested in meditation and liberation.

I would like to narrate a couple of events that I had discussed with Krishnaji. I had a strange out-of-body experience in Vasanta Vihar. I had finished my morning exercises and was lying flat on my back in *shavasana* (a relaxation posture in yoga). Suddenly I found myself floating on the roof. I could see my body lying inert on the ground. It passed after a few minutes. I told this to Krishnaji. He said such things happen naturally when one is sensitive but I should not think about it as a special "experience," and he told me to forget it.

I was a witness to a peculiar psychic phenomenon. I was sitting in his room talking about certain matters. Then there was a pause in the conversation. My mind must have wandered. A little later, he asked me whether I was thinking about such and such a person. I was surprised. I said "Yes, but Krishnaji, how did you know?" He said *"I saw the face of that person behind your head."* I wondered what it was. Was it a thought form? Materialization? I did not know. He did not say anything more or talk about it.

I used sometimes to argue with him. Once I was trying to convince him about some matter related to the Foundation, and he was saying something different. After a while he said, *"Stop arguing; listen to what I am telling you."* I then said, "Krishnaji, you are always telling us to listen, but you are not listening to me now." He put an end to my talk by saying lightly; *"I know what you are going to say."* It was as if he could read my mind. Then he said something revealing: *"Sunanda, people come to me with masks. They reveal only what they want to. It is up to them. I don't look behind their masks. It would be an invasion of privacy if one did it."* How extraordinarily sensitive he was. He seemed to imply that he could communicate with another only to the extent the other is open, vulnerable.

He used to talk to the trees and plants. He was so gentle. For a couple of years, some young trees were not growing well in Vasanta Vihar. He would talk to them: *"Come on, old lady, grow."* He seemed to have an extraordinary oneness with nature, trees, plants, and animals.

THE LIGHTER SIDE OF KRISHNAJI

KRISHNAJI WAS OCCASIONALLY FULL OF FUN. HE HAD A BANTERing relationship with me. He used to rag me, and would say, when I answered a question of his by shaking my head, *"Don't shake your head. One never knows whether you mean 'yes' or 'no.'"* Sometimes he would reveal this teasing side in his letters too. I quote relevant parts from three letters he wrote me that reveal this aspect of him.

Handwritten letter dated July 21, 1959
c/o Postmaster
Pahlgam, Kashmir

My dear Sunanda,
...Thank you very much for your letter, and it was nice of you to have
written, though I didn't know you had changed your name to Krishnaji!
You had signed your letter by that name...

J.K.

I was obviously absent-minded when I signed it that way. He had cut
out that portion of my letter to him where I had signed myself as Krishnaji
and enclosed it in his letter to me.

Sometimes I used to write to him about a book or an article that I had
read. After teaching in the university for a while, I had developed an
academic and complex way of writing. Here is a letter from him dated
March 2, 1975:

My dear Sunanda,
... I was so glad to get your letter, although it is a bit professorial.
Thank you for writing about the memory imprint and behavioral insight.
I think I catch the meaning, but I would like to have it explained in more
simple language. As I used to say to you, come down to my level and
explain what you mean. What you have said is important but I would
like to have it clearly explained because I see something which may
be my own or perhaps my distortion of the experts...

J.K.

Apart from "pulling my leg" about being abstruse and professorial,
it is overwhelming to see the utter humility that he had. He was an
extraordinary person.

I had learnt many things from observing him, from little things to the
extraordinary significance of being sensitive and caring for people. He
used to say that it was not enough to care for a person one day and then
forget him or her the next day. I had promised to write to him regularly
once a fortnight about all that was happening after I came to Vasanta
Vihar in 1976 and was looking after the Foundation affairs. Once I
delayed writing to him. His letter, dated April 5, 1979 from Ojai, says:

My dear Sunanda,

Mahomet has not come to the mountain, so the mountain must go to Mahomet. I have been wondering what is happening, as I haven't heard, and I wonder if you are ill, which I hope you are not...

J.K.

His sense of humor sometimes expressed itself in other ways: I liked to chew *pan* (betel leaf with some spices to help digestion), especially after a good, substantial meal. It so happened that one day I had taken a *pan* when Krishnaji was also present in the dining hall. He called for me and said, "*Sunanda, you don't go to a guru chewing pan! Go, throw it out and come.*" Everyone gathered around had a good laugh.

Krishnaji was a person who seemed to belong to both the East and the West and was at home in both the ambiences. At home, yes, and yet not. At a personal level, his lifestyle was different at these places. In India he wore the pajama-*kurta* every day and the traditional-style *dhoti* for the public talks. Soon after landing in India, he would put on Indian clothes. Once it so happened that his Indian clothes did not reach him on the day he arrived in Delhi, and he pulled me up for it. He was very particular about all such matters.

He was looked upon as a "guru" here in India. He was even referred to as a guru who was a non-guru. People fell at his feet. He did not discourage them, as he understood their background, but he was always shy when someone bowed down and touched his feet and showed their deep reverence in the traditional Indian style.

The lifestyle of his hosts everywhere, Eastern or Western, determined to a certain extent his activities. He could go for a walk or to a movie in the West, but going to a theater or a favorite restaurant was not possible in India. He was too well known. To that extent, such little freedoms, human as they are, were not to be for him in India.

In Ojai or Brockwood, he used to tell us that he met very few people outside the Foundation except for those who came to the gatherings. In India, his day-to-day engagements were very heavy. He met many more people in India and worked hard. Especially in the last years of his life, his schedule of talks, dialogues, and meeting people were much more than his frail body could bear. He had little time for himself except when he rested or wrote or went for walks. Many distinguished and eminent people met him and were often invited for lunch. He liked to meet such people and was deeply interested in knowing what was happening in India.

Since he always wore traditional Indian clothes here, I remember my first reaction after seeing him in a tracksuit at Brockwood. I could not imagine him in that dress, it was so alien to my image of him. There were no televisions in his rooms here, whether at Vasanta Vihar, Rajghat, or Rishi Valley. At Brockwood Park or Ojai he would spend quite some time watching "westerns." Those were his relaxations. In India he would read detective novels.

Perhaps he needed the two lifestyles, Western and Indian, two patterns and cultures, two different idioms of life. A part of him was Indian and another, Western. I had often observed that after a sufficiently long stay of two or three months in India, he would be eager to leave for Ojai or Brockwood Park. In a similar way, he would look forward to coming here after spending some time in the West. Where did he belong? To both? To neither?

From a very young age he had been brought up in the Western tradition, taught and cared for by British members of the Theosophical Society. His outward manner and behavior were Western, but he seemed to have retained at a deeper level the essence of the culture that he had been born into. The Indianness in him could be seen in little things: he liked listening to Sanskrit chants recited by orthodox brahman pandits, especially in Madras and Benares. He responded to Karnatic (South Indian) classical music, and we used to invite some of the most distinguished dancers and musicians to perform on the *vina*, flute, violin and *mridangam*. He appreciated the aesthetic traditions of this country. He told me in 1976 at Malibu, *"When you go back to India, have all the decorations done in Vasanta Vihar as they do in South India*—rangoli [traditional floor decorations made with white or colored powders], *coconuts, mango leaves strung together and the clay lights, incense and so on."* Right through the ten-year period from 1976 to 1986, every year before the talks began, we had those lovely traditional ornaments adorning the entrance gate at Vasanta Vihar.

NEW BEGINNINGS

MADRAS, 1986 / 1990

A NEW CHAPTER IN MY LIFE BEGAN. I SEE NOW HOW fortunate we were at leaving Vasanta Vihar at that point in time. Krishnaji was not there anymore. The leaving was a blessing in disguise. After being with him, to continue to work immediately with others under a different set of circumstances would have been difficult. It was an exit at the right time, though it was somewhat painful. When one is in the eye of the storm, one is caught, unable to extricate oneself. It is a little later that one realizes that a lack of awareness in oneself was responsible for many events. However, all these experiences gave me an inner strength and clarity of perception that helped me during the next decade of my life.

How true it is that after the passing away of a great teacher, students learn to stand on their own perceptions. I remember a conversation with Krishnaji in this connection. He was concerned about what the future would hold for some of us, and he remarked, *"Perhaps it is true that under a banyan tree nothing grows. K may be like that. When he is no more, two things could happen—either you will all peter out or grow up, come together."* I feel one has grown through the years. In small ways, each day small transformations happen during moments of awareness. There seems a greater authenticity in one's life that expresses itself in different and perceptible ways. A total transformation remains an idea that has yet to be realized. One has been a witness to a transformed life as that of K's, seen it, felt its sacred presence, but one has not lived or experienced it in oneself. But the vision of that transformation seems to ever invite and beckon one towards itself. And the only purpose that seems real now is to strive towards this elusive vision.

The years between 1986 and 1990 marked a period of withdrawal from the concerns of the Foundation. Though Pamaji and I were living in Madras, we were not involved in its activities.

The four years of our stay in Madras after Krishnaji's passing away were eventful and difficult and tested our inner strength and reliance. Four days after Krishnaji left for Ojai, on January 10, 1986, Pamaji developed an ischaemic heart condition. Five days later Achyutji had a myocardial infarction, and we both stayed with him in Bangalore until he recovered. Soon after that, Achyutji came to stay in Madras, as Radhaji had invited him to live in the Theosophical Society campus. When we left Vasanta Vihar, it was a total change for me. Many things coalesced.

Krishnaji passed away soon after, and not having a guiding spirit to help one on the path was a deep blow. I resigned from all the responsible positions like the secretary of the publications committee of the KFI and editor of the KFI bulletin. I had held these positions for seventeen years. All this happened within a month. It was almost like dying inwardly to the past. It was a complete ending of all the familiar activities and the known patterns. There was a vacuum, a wilderness, and an intense period of feeling lost. It was the most wholesome experience I have had of psychological death. There was nothing but emptiness. I felt that in some way I had let Krishnaji down, though what he wanted was nothing short of transformation, and I knew that was beyond my present capacities.

Pamaji, however, did not feel the same way as I did. He felt he had done whatever he could but was found inadequate by Krishnaji. He felt that he could not have done anything more than what he had done. It was not as though he did not feel the poignancy of what had happened. Perhaps he took a more pragmatic approach. He told me that he had asked Krishnaji at Rishi Valley whether it was only Vasanta Vihar that lacked the religious spirit, or whether Rishi Valley, Rajghat, Ojai, Brockwood Park, or any K place other than Vasanta Vihar had become "religious." Krishnaji had replied that none of the places had become religious, and added that Pamaji's concern should be with what was happening to himself. Krishnaji had this unique way of bringing one back to oneself and to one's own drawbacks and not allowing the person to make comparative statements. It was obviously the only integral approach.

Our life had a new beginning now. It was as though a whole past was wiped out and a new path had opened. We had a comfortable cottage near the sea and one another for companionship, in addition to our friends and well-wishers. Apart from all this, Achyutji was like a rock of stability. He gave us much affection and understanding, as he had throughout my life. It was a time for reflection and quietness, and we felt contentment. Small groups of people continued to visit and dialogue with us, and our inner search was the continuous glow that lighted our life.

New beginnings brought with them new challenges and trials. In 1987, Pamaji underwent bypass surgery. Then I became very seriously ill in 1989. During a routine colonoscopy, an accident occurred and there was a puncture. It developed into peritonitis. I went into an emergency operation; the specialists had given me less than five percent chance of recovery. For forty days I was in a state of coma, as both kidneys had failed. They put me on dialysis and a ventilator. The doctors felt I might not survive the illness. Somehow I was destined to live, perhaps for a purpose. It proved to be another turning point in my life.

After two months I came out of it all, almost unscathed but physically very frail. After three months of physiotherapy, I was almost back to normal. Pamaji had to bear the whole burden of my recovery during this period. Some of our close friends stood by us, and their presence helped us to see through these difficult times.

To help my convalescence, Radhaji graciously invited us to stay at the Olcott bungalow in the campus of the Theosophical Society. It was a beautiful century-old colonial-style structure with large grounds facing the sea. Living in these serene surroundings, I recovered my health and spirit gradually. For hours I used to lie on an easy chair in the verandah, listening to the sound of the sea and the songs of the many birds that had made their homes there. Ancient trees surrounding the bungalow cocooned me in their healing silence. Achyutji lived close to us, and the shared companionship gave me a great strength. It was a period of quiet retreat and contemplation. The pain of leaving Vasanta Vihar had disappeared, and I was able to look at the past calmly, without judgment. And I felt I had been given another chance.

The following year, 1990, we moved our residence from Madras to Pune. We had decided that we had to choose a place where we could settle down for the final years of our lives. Pune seemed the best alternative, for we had many relatives and friends there.

PUNE, 1992

LOOKING BACK, I DO FEEL THAT DESTINY PLAYED ITS HAND once again in our moving to Pune, as it did in the year of 1947 when I first met Krishnaji, and again in 1975 when we went to Vasanta Vihar. We had no idea or plan to carry out any major responsibilities on behalf of the Foundation. We had come a full circle, for Pune was where we had married and settled down in 1949.

In May 1990, we began the construction of our new home. By September of that year, a proposal to start a co-educational residential school was proposed. Achyutji was very keen that a K school should be established in western India. For nearly four decades Krishnaji had talked in Bombay and Pune, and people from all over this region had listened to his talks. There was a current of receptivity and the right psychological soil for a school of this kind. Between 1990 and 1992, three or four proposals were initiated and lands located, but due to some impediment or other, they didn't work out. In April 1992, the present land where the Sahyadri School is now located was donated to the KFI by Shri N. K. Firodia, an eminent industrialist.

Achyutji, Firodia, and Pamaji launched the project with this beautiful land of ninety acres located on a hilltop overlooking the waters of the Bhima River. The site was at a distance of sixty-five kilometers from Pune. Within three months of launching the project, fate struck another blow — our beloved Achyutji passed away. It now fell upon the frail shoulders of Pamaji, who was nearing eighty, to take on the full responsibility of completing this project, with me playing the supportive role.

The project was accomplished against great odds. Financial backing had to be obtained, basic infrastructure like roads, power, and water had to be developed, and most of all, the right people to manage and direct the school had to be found. A road leading uphill to the school had to be constructed. Water had to be pumped up from the lake to a height of 500 feet; electrical and telephone cables had to be provided. It took nearly two years to create and complete these infrastructures. The place was finally ready, and Sahyadri School was inaugurated on September 10, 1995, in the birth centenary year of Krishnaji.

The school has gained a very good reputation in a short time and is growing rapidly and gaining in strength and stability. Today, it has 260 girls and boys in residence with a staff of thirty-seven teachers.

A VISION FOR THE SAHYADRI SCHOOL

OUR VISION FOR THE SCHOOL WAS INSPIRED IN SPIRIT BY Krishnaji's intentions for the schools. How did Krishnaji regard the schools? He saw them as vehicles to spread the teaching and a place for seekers to live together in a community of like-minded people to dialogue and share insights. Krishnaji gave of himself and his energy, concern, and time to the schools while in India, especially to Rishi Valley and Rajghat, which have now been in existence for more than fifty years.

I vividly remember a discussion on the opening of the new schools[21] on December 31, 1974. At that time, some schools wanted to be affiliated to the KFI schools. We were all against adding any more schools, as we felt it meant more responsibilities and that we should first create the right soil in the already existing schools. Krishnaji asked us to look at it slightly differently: "*Don't go on saying that Rishi Valley and Rajghat come first; we have to establish the roots here first. Maybe you can have two schools run under the auspices of the Foundation if they want to join you. Then you will have the responsibility to direct them, go there, push the teachers, call all the teachers together, hold meetings, and keep the flame going. Because you don't have the flame, you say, 'Let us confine ourselves to Rishi Valley and Rajghat.' If the flames are there in the Foundation, anew, then the more you spread, the greater will it spread.*" A question was asked whether it was as easy as he thought, for we might find ourselves in a mess later. Krishnaji felt that this was not the right spirit. "*The flame has to be alive. It has to be kindled, kept going by meeting the teachers, going to the centers, talking to them, pushing them.*" This in itself, he felt, would bring an energy that would spread.

Krishnaji's involvement with the schools began in an intensive way in 1948 with the Rajghat Besant School and continued till his last visit to Rishi Valley in 1985, just a few weeks before he died. Year after year he visited these places, stayed for a few weeks, talked to the students, and had long discussions with the teachers. He was interested in everything, from the type of food given to the students and the clothing they wore to the crops cultivated and trees planted, and the help and educational facilities extended to the poor in the villages around.

Krishnaji had given guidelines to schools on two fronts. One concerned creating the right ambience in order to bring about a different kind of mind, and the other was with regard to the nature of the organization that would manage the place. He wanted to create a deeply religious ambience and envisaged the schools as oases or little pockets of sanity in a world that was increasingly becoming dangerous to live in, a world torn apart by violence and wars, separatism and hate, into national, ethnic, religious, and sectarian divisions.

He felt that a new generation brought up differently in such an ambience would grow up to be good human beings. He held that the school should view everything else, such as excellence in academics and acquisition of other skills, as secondary to this primary purpose. The primary intent must be to help students feel a sense of sanctity for human existence and the manifested world with all its beings. He tried to help the teachers and others who were responsible for the school to see the importance of being rooted in self-knowledge. This was essential in order to create an atmosphere where there was freedom from fear and pressure. In such an environment, he felt, children would learn and be alive with curiosity, listening to the songs of birds, the music of the winds, and the myriad whispers of the universe. It is only then, he felt, that children would listen with care to another human being, to their peers, teachers, parents, and others. In such a listening there can come about a change in the subtlety of the mind and create an affective movement of the heart.

With regard to the organization, it seemed to me that he chose and trusted one individual in the school to take decisions. In order that the schools function democratically, he insisted on establishing a core group that would take consensual decisions through dialogue and discussion. There was to be no hierarchy, no authority based on a psychological sense of the superior and inferior between those working in the place. There was to be only functional authority and not the authority born of status. Functional authority had to be exercised with competence, as no organization could function with order and efficiency without it. Only in exceptional cases would the head of the school take overriding decisions. Periodically, it happened that when the person in whom Krishnaji had vested this trust failed to live up to the expectations, he or she left the place.

The school was therefore not to be just an organization. What would make the place alive and different was to be the spirit of self-awareness on the part of individuals. And this had to be attempted by a group of teachers working together. When this spirit of togetherness operated, problems, issues, misunderstandings, and all manner of decisions could be taken up and dealt with. There would then be a flow of awareness permeating the classrooms and playfields, interpersonal relationships, and organizational matters.

I feel there is a core group of teachers in each of the schools who are committed to the teaching, and their insights inspired by Krishnaji have taken roots and set forth new directions.

THE STUDY CENTER:
A VISION FOR A
NEW MIND

I PERSONALLY FELT A LITTLE FAR AWAY FROM ALL THE HECTIC activities that went into developing the school. I felt that the real cornerstone of the school should be the study center. Krishnaji held that the study center should be the heart of every school to inspire the community through continuous dialogue and inquiry.

Krishnaji felt that there was a tremendous urgency for creating study centers for adults in each one of the K places. He held that these religious places should become beacons of light in the years to come. He raised many issues. *"How do they become truly religious places? How does a physical place become sacred space? What is the ambience that will hold the sacred?"*

He spoke against regimentation in religious organizations, and he wanted these study centers to be different from the existing patterns of ashrams. He had great respect for the *sannyasi*, the wandering mendicant or monk. He would be extremely courteous and affectionate to such people personally, but he used to say that in India they represented a value and a way of life that was losing its significance.

By 1980 or thereabouts, Krishnaji started feeling that there were too many schools and that very little had been done to create an ashram or a study center. In his conversations with me, he used the word *ashrama* in the beginning; later he toyed with the name "neo-ashrama" but then changed it to a study center. He felt that the very word *ashrama* had traditional connotations, for it was too much a part of the Hindu consciousness, and would evoke a patterned response.

Krishnaji spoke at length about his vision for a study center (dictated to me by Krishnaji at Vasanta Vihar on January 26/27, 1984):

They [these centers] *must last a thousand years, unpolluted, like a river that has the capacity to cleanse itself; which means no authority whatsoever for the inhabitants. And the teaching in themselves have the authority of the truth. It is a place for the flowering of goodness, where there is a communication and cooperation not based on work, an ideal, or personal authority. Cooperation implies not around some object or principle, belief, and so on, but a sharing of insights. As one comes to the place, each one in his work, working in the garden or doing something [else], may discover something as he is working. He communicates and has a dialogue with the other inhabitants, to be questioned and doubted in order to see the weight of the truth of his discovery. So there is a constant communication and not a solitary achievement, a solitary enlightenment or understanding. It is the responsibility of each one to bring about this sense—that if each one of us discovers something basic anew, it is not personal but it is for all people who are there to share.*

It is not a community. The very word 'community' or 'commune' is an aggressive or separative movement [away] from the whole of humanity. But it does not mean that the whole humanity comes into this place. It is essentially a religious center according to what K has said about religion. It is a place where not only is one physically active but there is a sustained and continuous inward watching. So there is a movement of learning where each one becomes the teacher and the disciple. It is not a place for one's own illumination or one's own goal of fulfillment, artistically, religiously, or in any other way, but rather a place for sustaining and nourishing one another to flower in goodness.

This is not a place for romanticists or sentimentalists. This requires a good brain, which does not mean an intellectual but a brain that is objective, is fundamentally honest to itself, and has integrity in word and deed.

This place must be of great beauty, with trees, birds, and quiet, for beauty is truth and truth is goodness and love. The external beauty, external tranquillity, and silence may affect the inner tranquillity, but the environment must in no way influence the inner beauty. Beauty can only be when the self is not; the environment, which must have great wonder, must in no way be an absorbing factor like a child's toy. Here, there are no toys but inner depths, substance, and integrity that is not put together by thought.

At the end of his life, K was deeply concerned with the nature of relationship between people who came together to explore what a religious mind was. What does it mean to lead a religious life? How does a *sangha* [spiritual fellowship] come about? Whenever people come together, live together in a study center, how do they move together in perception? He spoke to the members of the Foundation a great deal about it. He was passionately pointing out the need to love, share, and be a light unto oneself.

If we look at all that he has spoken and written about study centers, we get certain insights and guidelines, a certain direction in which to feel our way towards working it out.

First, a study center is not a community. There are no permanent inhabitants. When people live permanently in such a place, it generally becomes a community with its hierarchical, dependent nature of relationship and routines and ritualized way of meditation and living. This was totally against his vision. Here people come for a short stay, for a few weeks, and go back with a deep awakening to meet life anew.

One goes to a study center to study Krishnaji's teaching; then one reflects on what has been read or listened to, in order to understand and observe the movement of motivations, desire, conflict within: in short, to observe the way the self operates.

Those who come to stay need to work out their day intelligently, in terms of leisure for reflection, meditation, and being in silence. It is also necessary to do some work, maybe in the garden, kitchen, or any place where help is required. Dialogues with others form an important aspect of communication and help to come upon insights. Dialogues, introspection, work, and meditation give a new orientation to life. Each one has to discover his or her needs and go deeper into realms hitherto unknown to oneself about one's consciousness. There is no guru to guide, no hierarchy, no conformity, and no pattern of behavior. There is no group therapy or confessional. How does such a group shape itself? This is a question to live and experiment with. There are no tailored or ready-made answers. What is important to grasp is an urgency to have a creative and affectionate relationship between people who thus come together.

Such a place is aesthetically built, with a sense of beauty and a natural loveliness. Such places are sheltered from the marketplace of worldly life and are like oases. When a person comes to such a place, the moment he or she steps into it, the burdens, worries, problems, and fears that the person carries naturally stop, even though temporarily.

The Sahyadri Study Centre, with a room for study and meditation, was formally inaugurated on November 29, 1998. It is a unique and beautiful structure. There is an office, a cafeteria, and five cottages for visitors to live in. It is a place of great beauty, overlooking the undulating Sahyadri Mountains and the valley where the Bhima River flows and merges into a lake. As one enters the place, a feeling of a vast unlimited space, a profound silence, and a sense of sanctity strike one. Sunsets and sunrises are extraordinarily beautiful, and the mind naturally falls into a state of inner quietness.

A SENSE OF COMPLETION

AS I LOOK BACK, CERTAIN FACTORS STRIKE ME AS SIGNIFICANT about the way the projects started, developed, and were completed. Pamaji had to face many difficulties single-handedly—hundreds of details during the construction, times of financial shortages, myriad other problems of coordination and management. At that time we thought of what Krishnaji had often told us: *"Do the right thing, Sir. Money and support will come."* It happened that way. Some donors offered their generous support, and the KFI schools came up with timely loans at low interest. And above all, something from within oneself brought energy to help us to carry on the task. It was primarily, I feel, a deep conviction or one could call it faith in furthering Krishnaji's work. One considers contributing towards the creation of such a school and study center to be a purifying and sacred task. This belief and feeling kept Pamaji going, despite his advanced years. We shared all the trials and the reward of completion together. There was a continual feeling within us that it was not our efforts or the group's alone that made it all possible. We felt that the benediction of K's memories and presence played a central role in this work.

THE PRESENT

WHEN I REFLECT UPON ALL THAT HAS HAPPENED TO ME DURING the last four or five years, two things appear to be significant. One is the recovery or rebirth I had after my illness in 1989/1990. It seems as though I had to live in order to play a crucial part in the starting of the Sahyadri School and Study Centre. Both places are moving well on their own momentum, and capable young persons are directing their course. The task has been completed, and there is a sense of fulfillment and a feeling that a new role awaits me.

The second factor was that the nature of my involvement in Sahyadri was quite different from the one at Vasanta Vihar earlier. I have not been in the center of things here. There has been no self-projection or a false sense of importance. There was, from the beginning, an inward detachment, the feeling that I had an anonymous role to play and that I must do it quietly. The task did not take root psychologically, in the sense that one felt like an outsider while being fully committed to it. It has been a renewing and refreshing experience.

The project, however, affected me at a different level. The whole enterprise was so immense that with meager financial resources and other constraints and challenges there was a continual feeling of anxiety. I was assailed by doubts: Would the school start in the birth centenary year of Krishnaji as publicly announced? Would we able to find the right people? Such tensions do take a heavy toll of one's energy and health. My already ailing body deteriorated still further. When one is watchful of oneself, it is fascinating to observe how these worries and trepidation arise and dissolve. I am now left with an overall feeling that in some measure one has been responsible for the birth and growth of Sahyadri School and Study Centre.

Where am I now? Where lies the quest for the sacred with which one started the journey? The quest seems to have led me to an existence that is acquiring a quality of non-selfishness. The quest continues in discovering the true nature of one's consciousness and ending fragmentation. This is what I have been seeking ever since I began my search many years ago. During this long passage of time, I have gone through many experiences and learnt from authentic insights about my life and the very meaning of human existence. As I observe my journey now, I see certain trends. There is the urgency for the quest to end, but it is not merely an idealistic wish. I am no longer seeking transformation. If I had ever thought of and sought after a K consciousness, such a desire is not with me anymore. I have seen that it is an illusion to seek it. There is no ideal consciousness that I am longing for, and I know with certainty that all seeking is in time. There is only the quest to end one's conditioning, and there is an urgency to work at it. The timeless, I know, cannot be thought of so long as seeking for it continues, whether grossly or subtly.

The fabric of mind as it is has not transcended time. One is somewhere in between. I am reminded of what Krishnaji once said to me humorously: *"We are not enlightened, but neither are we unenlightened!"* Does it mean that one gives up the deep intention of ending conditioning and all the dualities within the mind? Not at all! On the contrary, that is the work that needs to be done till one lives. It is not a matter of moving towards a goal from which one does not return. With the understanding I have of the way, I know that there is no seeking it or reaching out for it. So what is significant now is the actual movement of awareness towards insights into the confusion and conflicts of daily life. They express themselves in many ways, in one's responses to people and events.

One of the dominant tendencies of the mind is to think about either past events and experiences or future ones. My mind does not bring up memories from the past so often as before, and if they do come up, there does not seem to be much emotional content. Anxieties about the future do come more often; for instance, thoughts about my crippled and weak body do overtake me and I wonder, "Will I become more ill, more handicapped, and constantly dependent on others for daily living?" These thoughts of what will happen tomorrow create great anxiety and fear in me. Krishnaji's statement that "thought is fear" is not just an aphorism to me but is part of my authentic perception of life's experiences. It lies within one's capacity to allow the clouds of thoughts to pass through without resistance, for then the clouds are no more. After a while, this meditative awareness becomes self-sustaining, and I am less paralyzed by such thoughts.

I remember an insightful advice given by Krishnaji as early as 1976. Krishnaji, Mary Zimbalist, and I were at Malibu. At lunch the discussion turned to aging and people having serious handicaps and illnesses. I exclaimed that I would not like to live much longer if I became handicapped or paralyzed. His response was rather strange. He said, *"What arrogance! There are millions of people physically and mentally handicapped and deprived. You cannot dictate terms to life. Whatever comes, face it intelligently."* An intelligent acceptance without resistance such as self-pity or depression means to be with the actual situation without escaping from it. In doing that, one can face it afresh each time. This awareness gives one the inner strength to live with ailments with a sense of humor and tolerance. One has to face aging, ailments, and the many problems that come one's way till the end of one's life. The quality of the mind's awareness and alertness to itself will determine the quality of one's daily life. The quest is to deepen this intelligence of awareness and learn a way of living in the present.

I remember again an occasion when almost in despair I asked Krishnaji why he could not transform me. He said, *"I can't. You have to do it yourself. Learn from everything in life."* At another time he had said, *"Don't ask to be transformed. K has come not to transform but to awaken."* Certainly, he has awakened human consciousness; so many millions have listened to him, read his works, and been awakened to a new way of perceiving and living. It is clear to me now that one's life could only be directed towards the sacred through a radical transformation of my consciousness. However, total transformation does not seem to come through wish nor through the kind of practice one has rendered so far. If it happens, it happens. The foundation of right living and right attention alone seems to be the only sure ground that one has to travel on. And awakened by K, one walks on that path in a continuing journey of discovery and learning.

The journey of the self towards the sacred is exacting but also in a sense inevitable. Through the years, the journey has undergone many stages and seen many changes. Over the years, meditative reflection has made the self a loose entity. It seems to appear and disappear. When it disappears, consciousness changes. At such times, the heart speaks, one's sensitivity gets heightened, and relationships seem to flow naturally without blocks. The journey is no longer a movement either. It is the stopping of the journey, the stopping of the movement of the self, that is the summation of my life's quest, at any given moment today.

This is, however, not the total transformation that Krishnaji talks about when he says, *"Where you are, the 'other' is not,"* or, *"The Known and the Unknown can never meet,"* or again, *"Once you are on the other shore there is no coming and going."* There are no approximations to these states; all that I can be is to be less and less caught in the web of selfishness, and the self and its trap.

Talking of traps, Krishnaji once remarked to me, *"The world is a trap. You are in the trap. You are the trap. Don't speak to it. Then you are out of the trap."* It was like a Zen *koan*. What I understood of that statement was that any self-dialogue is still divisive of consciousness, and so we have to deeply understand how we are the creators of our own trap. What remains is to be in meditation and allow such states to visit and leave the rest.

As Krishnaji says:

"Meditation is not a search; it's not a seeking, a probing, an exploration. It is an explosion and discovery. It's not the taming of the brain to conform nor is it a self-introspective analysis. It is certainly not the training in concentration, which includes, chooses, and denies....It is the total emptiness of the brain....It is out of this emptiness that love comes....It's the end and beginning of all things.

"Meditation is the emptying of consciousness, not to receive, but to be empty of all endeavor. There must be space for stillness, not the space created by thought and its activities but that space that comes through denial and destruction, when there is nothing left of thought and its projection. In emptiness alone can there be creation."

Salutations to the eternal teaching.

A F T E R W O R D

SUNANDA PATWARDHAN PASSED AWAY SOON AFTER SHE HAD completed a first draft of this book. The prolonged illness that began in 1989 had progressively worsened. The final weeks were very painful, but she decided not to opt for any life support systems and courageously faced the alternative. She continued to meet her friends and family with a poise and dignity that was very moving. Her last wish was that she be able to continue her spiritual journey in the next life, fulfilling the quest that she had begun in this lifetime.

ENDNOTES

1. Annie Besant (1847–1933) was a British free thinker, champion of women's rights, trade unionism, and birth control. She became president of the Theosophical Society in 1907, and in India founded the Benares Hindu University and the Congress Party. Until her death, she was a supporter of Krishnamurti's destiny of being a teacher for the world. He thought of Mrs. Besant as his adopted mother, and cherished her memory through his life.

2. Pupul Jayakar, considered one of the doyennes of Indian culture, was the culture minister under Indira Gandhi's regime and contributed greatly to revitalizing the handloom and handicrafts industry in India. She has written a well-received biography on Krishnamurti.

3. Nandini Mehta is the sister of Pupulji. She was a member of the KFI and manages the Bal Anand, an after-school learning center for children from underprivileged homes in Bombay.

4. S. Balasundaram is a member of the KFI and was the principal of Rishi Valley for seventeen years, until 1975.

5. G. Narayan was a member of the KFI and was the principal and director of Rishi Valley until 1984.

6. D. Rajagopal had been long associated with Krishnaji, from the time he left the Theosophical Society. He tried to gain control over Krishnaji's properties and publications, but this was thwarted by the KFA.

7. Shiva Rao was the assistant editor of Annie Besant's well-known political paper, *New India*. He was a distinguished journalist and a member of the Indian Parliament.

8. Dr. David Bohm was one of the most eminent physicists of the time. He had a close relationship with Krishnaji and participated in many dialogues with him. Some of the most illuminating are his video dialogues with Krishnaji, which explore the nature of reality and truth in philosophy and science, emphasizing the importance of insight in understanding the limits of thought. Some of the more important dialogues have been published in the collection, *The Ending of Time*.

9. Indira Gandhi, who was prime minister of India at that time and one of the most controversial figures on the Indian political scene, had met Krishnaji several times and had great reverence for him.

10. Erna Lilliefelt was the secretary of KFA for many years. She was in charge of the various court cases against KWINC that sought to regain various properties and copyrights belonging to Krishnaji from KWINC.

11. Mary Zimbalist was a very close associate of Krishnaji, and a senior trustee of KFA and KFT. From 1967, she was Krishnaji's hostess in Ojai and Brockwood Park and took care of him.

12. Dr. David Shainberg was a leading psychiatrist in New York City. He participated with Dr. David Bohm and other scientists in video dialogues with Krishnaji. He arranged several seminars for Krishnaji in New York.

13. Dr. Briggs is a professor of English who has published several popular books on science and literature.

14. Dr. Sudarshan is a particle physicist at the University of Texas interested in exploring the common ground between religion and science.

15. Radha Burnier is the International President of the Theosophical Society. She is also a trustee of the KFI and KTM. She has had a close association with Krishnaji. She writes and travels all over the world, giving talks on Theosophy.

16. Prema Srinivasan comes from a distinguished industrial house. She is well known for her contributions in the arena of culture. She was closely associated with Krishnaji and the work at Vasanta Vihar. She has been a trustee of the KFI for many years.

17. Padma Santhanam and her husband, R. S. Santhanam, belong to an eminent industrial house. They were responsible for the growth and development of "The School, KFI," Madras. Mrs. Padma Santhanam was very supportive of the work at Vasanta Vihar.

18. Professor Jagan Nath Upadhyaya (1921–1986) was trained as a traditional Vedanta Acharya and a Brahmin priest. The voice of dissent in him urged him to take to the study and practice of Buddhist philosophy and tantra. He published many papers in learned journals in Sanskrit and Hindi, and edited a critical edition of *Vimalprabha Tika* and a commentary on the *Kala-Chakra-Tantra*. He had dialogues with Krishnamurti between 1974 and 1985 at Rajghat, Varanasi.

19. C. W. Leadbeater was a Theosophist and a close associate of Annie Besant.

20. H. P. Blavatsky, along with Col. Henry Olcott, founded the Theosophical Society in 1875, in the United States. She was an extraordinary clairvoyant and mystic. Her book, *The Secret Doctrine*, was the foundation on which the occult school of Theosophy was established.

21. The KFI manages the following schools: Rishi Valley in Andhra Pradesh, Rajghat at Benares, Bal Anand at Bombay, The School in Madras, the Valley School at Bangalore, the Bhagirathi Valley School in Uttar Kashi, and the Sahyadri School near Pune.

$\mathcal{B}$ooks in the series of memoirs
published by $\mathcal{E}$dwin House $\mathcal{P}$ublishing, Inc.

The Kitchen Chronicles: 1001 Lunches with
J. Krishnamurti by Michael Krohnen

As the River Joins the Ocean: Reflections about
J. Krishnamurti by G. Narayan

The Transparent Mind: A Journey with Krishnamurti
by Ingram Smith

A Vision of the Sacred: My Personal Journey with
Krishnamurti by Sunanda Patwardhan